MAKE IT *in* CHINA

The 6 Secrets to Successful Sourcing

STEVE FENIGER

Candid Creation Publishing

First published 2018

Copyright © 2018 Steve Feniger

All rights reserved. No part of this publication may be reproduced, stored in a retrieval system, or transmitted, in any form or by any means, electronic, mechanical, photocopying, recording or otherwise, without the prior permission of the publisher, except for inclusion of brief quotations in a review.

Candid Creation Publishing books are available through most major bookstores in Singapore. For bulk order of our books at special quantity discounts, please email us at enquiry@candidcreation.com.

MAKE IT IN CHINA
The 6 Secrets to Successful Sourcing

Author	: Steve Feniger
Cover Illustration	: Steve Feniger
Publisher	: Phoon Kok Hwa
Editor	: Tansey Tang
Cover Designer	: Ryanne Ng
Layout	: Corrine Teng
Published by	: Candid Creation Publishing LLP
	167 Jalan Bukit Merah
	#05-12 Connection One Tower 4
	Singapore 150167
Tel/Fax	: (65) 6273 7623
Website	: www.candidcreation.com
Facebook	: www.facebook.com/CandidCreationPublishing
Email	: enquiry@candidcreation.com
ISBN	: 978-981-11-6438-5

National Library Board, Singapore Cataloguing in Publication Data

Names: Feniger, Steve.
Title: Make it in China : the 6 secrets to successful sourcing / Steve Feniger.
Other titles: Six secrets to successful sourcing
Description: Singapore : Candid Creation Publishing LLP, 2018.
Identifiers: OCN 1022117465 | 978-981-11-6438-5 (paperback)
Subjects: LCSH: Contracting out--China. | Contracting out--Management. | Business planning.
Classification: DDC 658.40580951--dc23

Dedicated to my wife Eve and our twins Jasmine and Justine, who gave me purpose.

ACKNOWLEDGEMENTS

With acknowledgements and thanks to:

- My board—John, Sandeep, Craig, and Wai;
- My mentors—Bernie, Steve, and Dave;
- My friends who acted as "beta readers", improving my story whilst providing endless encouragement—my Mother, my Sister, Bernie, Don John, Homer, fellow-author Wai, Sandeep, Craig;
- The multiple clients who invited me into their businesses and became personal friends.

CONTENTS

Foreword vii
Preface xi

Introduction: Why China? 1
Secret 1: Generating Trust 31
Secret 2: Mastering Negotiation 43
Secret 3: Networking with Purpose 63
Secret 4: Building your Platform 81
Secret 5: Partnering for Profit 103
Secret 6: Coping with Challenges 117
Conclusion 141

Afterword 143
Works Cited 147
About 55 Consulting 151

FOREWORD

Ever since Marco Polo told his story, overseas audiences have enjoyed gaining insight from travellers with experience of China. When China started to open up in the late 1970s, quite a few pioneering traders and investors turned authors and continued this tradition. In the 1990s and 2000s in particular, bookshelves started to fill with more and more volumes offering tips, analysis, advice, and anecdotes about doing business in rising and reforming China. However, the pace of change in China is so great that, if you pick up many of these books today, you might think they were talking about a different country. It was a land of power outages, with a shortage of decent hotels, bewildering bureaucratic hurdles, and a reputation for being unfathomable to outsiders.

We are now in the late 2010s. Today, urban China in particular is a modern society with metros and high-speed rails, gleaming commercial buildings, some world-class personal and business services, and a sizable and growing middle class familiar with global brands and lifestyles.

This reflects the rapid development of China as a leading producer of goods and as a market. The challenges for outsiders doing business in China have changed significantly. At the same time, the rewards for those able to grasp the opportunities have grown massively.

Steve Feniger came to Asia in the 1990s from the UK as a well-seasoned buyer of clothing for a major British and international retail chain. This was a time when China was just about to take off as a manufacturing export hub—a development that would have a major, historic impact on the global supply chain and the world economy.

Steve's career path led him to the forefront of this revolution in sourcing. He went on to manage global sourcing for a major US company, with responsibilities that extended to the manufacturing operations. He was one of the people who made that globalisation boom a reality. After continued success, including leading a sourcing company and taking it public, he went into consulting—and, as this book shows, writing.

Make It in China makes full use of Steve's experience doing business in China. This naturally concerns sourcing—which is still one of the main reasons Western business people come to China, and will remain a major economic role of the country in the foreseeable future. His expertise in manufacturing and buying is evident from the book.

But the lessons of this book apply to any line of business in China today.

China has developed and integrated with the world far more quickly and deeply than anyone would have imagined in the 1990s. China's own business people have learned, experimented, adapted—and it is probably true to say that they and their overseas clients have matured. Chinese entrepreneurs and managers know more about the world than they did 20 years ago, and vice versa.

China still has unique characteristics, thanks to major factors such as its geography and its culture. China has come a long way, but that does not mean it has become more Western. Anyone wanting to do business there—not only from the West but even from Hong Kong—needs to be aware of the differences in business style, personal relationships, and more formal issues like regulation and officialdom in the Mainland. Steve has lived and worked in this rapidly shifting environment, and his book has a lot to offer anyone interested in social as well as business relationships between Mainlanders and outsiders today.

Although China has its own rich national—and indeed regional—cultures, doing business across boundaries comes down to the same basic ideas that all humans share. Some of Steve's most valuable insights reflect on the building of trust and the importance of integrity. Anyone from any background can learn from his thoughts on these fundamentals.

Make It in China is not simply about doing business in China, but about the changes that China as a whole is going through. The author makes some thought-provoking, and in some cases perhaps provocative, points about the way the country is developing as a global economic presence. These issues are the subject of much debate today. More so than many commentators, Steve Feniger has deep experience to support his views and to share with the reader.

The Honourable Bernard Charnwut Chan
Convenor of Hong Kong Executive Council
Hong Kong Deputy to the National People's Congress of People's Republic of China
President of Asia Financial Holdings

PREFACE

> "You cannot open a book without learning something."
>
> Confucius

On Sunday, 21 April 1996, my birthday wish came true. As I turned 37 years old, I got off a plane from London and entered Hong Kong, not as a visitor, but as a new resident. Excited to be escaping my corporate rut in London, I'd volunteered to spend two years in Hong Kong. I'd frequently visited for short business trips, but this time it was different. Change was in the air—Hong Kong's handover from Britain to the People's Republic of China was a year away, and no one knew how it would play out.

Walking into the offices of Marks & Spencer Asia the next day, I was immediately struck by the superficial similarities with the 4,000-strong Head Office in London, as well as the underlying strangeness of its culture. I asked the first few Chinese staff I met if they had enjoyed a pleasant weekend. They replied, "I was bored," or "I slept the whole time and did nothing!" I wasn't seriously enquiring about their time off; just making small talk. This was my first lesson in understanding the more literal approach in the Orient.

It was only when I started learning Cantonese that I better understood my colleagues' perspective. There are no words for "yes" or "no" in Cantonese—The question, "Have you eaten?" is answered with either, "I have eaten," or "I haven't eaten." The different language reflects different thinking. It's not better or worse, just different.

How did I end up in Hong Kong? I was fortunate to spend the first 20 years of my career, straight from university, working as a clothing buyer for the large British retailer Marks & Spencer, who proudly bought most of their clothing from UK-based suppliers. I was dispatched to Hong Kong in 1996 to develop a lower-cost sourcing model that involved buying direct from Asian manufacturers, both for the UK "mother ship" of 300 stores and the fledgling Asian retail business, which was operating in six different countries in the Orient.

My work in Hong Kong, which demonstrated the significant savings in cost and potential improvements in quality that were available by "going direct", was not well received by the board of directors. To be blunt, it was ignored. They were very married to the loyal UK manufacturers, and preferred them to set up import operations and act as middlemen for Far Eastern vendors, to subsidise their struggling UK factories. The cost savings available by manufacturing in Asia were being drained off by these suppliers, and not accessed by Marks & Spencer to either lower their retail prices and become more competitive, or improve margins. By then, I had seen the light, and realised that there was a sourcing world outside of Marks & Spencer that I needed to access, and a base in Hong Kong that I enjoyed more than London.

I became obsessed with working for a US company. I figured that since I had already been working for the premier and largest UK retailer, there was little point changing jobs for more of the same. It was time to strike out and experience what I regarded as the global centre of excellence for my industry. After 19 years with just one company, I feared complacency and regret at only having worked in one institution more than the fear of failure if my career didn't work out elsewhere! So, in 2008, I challenged myself to find a Hong Kong-based sourcing job working for a respected US company.

Fortunately, the reputation of Marks & Spencer for the high quality of both its products and managers was still in the ascendancy 20 years ago, and several large Chinese vendors recommended me as a capable and honest sourcing expert to their US clients. I immediately received an offer to be the Senior Vice President of Global Sourcing for Warnaco, a Fortune 500-listed US company that owned or licensed brands including Calvin Klein Jeans, Calvin Klein Underwear, Chaps Ralph Lauren, and Speedo North America.

The culture in Warnaco was very "hire and fire", and after nine months, the Global Head of Manufacturing was terminated, and I was given the additional responsibility of running all of Warnaco's factories across China, Sri Lanka, the Philippines, Mexico, and Honduras. This turned out to be a fantastic opportunity. Warnaco did about 30% of its own production (the balance was sourced from third-party factories by my team in Asia), but I didn't have a clue what was involved in the process. I'd visited hundreds of factories, but only to assess, criticise, and beat them down on price. Suddenly, I was responsible for filling factories and ensuring their profitability. It was daunting stuff, but the lessons I learnt transformed my understanding of sourcing, and more importantly, allowed me to connect with factory owners in a way I previously couldn't. To this day, every time I visit a new supplier, I make a point of sharing with the owner that I have run multiple factories.

In 2001, after a gruelling three years at Warnaco, I was headhunted to take over as CEO of a buying agency that then issued an IPO on the Hong Kong Stock Exchange in 2002. With 38 offices across Asia, this agency presented a steep learning curve, and the challenges of managing a publicly listed company impacted every aspect of running the company. After five years as CEO, I left corporate life to set up my own buying office in Shanghai, and developed my consulting business, which is still going strong.

WHY I WROTE THIS BOOK

Ten years ago, I started giving talks at conferences in Shanghai and Hong Kong to CEOs who wanted a simple guide to doing business in the Orient. Interest focused on how to deal with corruption, protecting intellectual property rights, hiring the right staff, setting up offices, and choosing the right business structure. I enjoyed sharing my many mistakes with my peers, and found that my consulting business benefited from these talks. The more I shared *what* to do in a wide variety of situations, the more they wanted help with *how* to do it. However, I was only able to share with a limited number of people.

In recent years, my friends and colleagues have been lobbying for me to share my experiences in China with a wider audience by writing a book, in part because they find my anecdotes, experiences, and career surreal, and in part because they feel those starting businesses in China are frequently unprepared.

THE STRUCTURE OF THIS BOOK

After the introductory chapter, which explores why China should be front and centre in your business strategy, I discuss the 6 Secrets to Successful Sourcing in individual chapters:

1. Generating Trust
2. Mastering Negotiation
3. Networking with Purpose
4. Building your Platform
5. Partnering for Profit
6. Coping with Challenges

Each Secret is introduced with a story about a fictional CEO called Wes, an American businessman who has dabbled with sourcing his clothing and holiday products from China, and who has recently gotten serious and is spending much more time in Hong Kong and Mainland China. We will see the challenges Wes's business is facing, and the decisions he is making in order to make his sourcing business in China successful.

Each Secret chapter then explores the Lessons to be Learnt from Wes's situation, and concludes with a Summary of the Key Points.

Now, it's time to explore working in China.

INTRODUCTION: WHY CHINA?

> We are not jealous of others' success and we will not complain about others who have benefited. We will welcome them aboard the express train of Chinese development.
>
> President Xi Jinping, 2017

China's eclipse of the US as the world's largest economy is not a question of if, but when. There will be bumps along the way, but China is an arrow pointing up for the foreseeable future, and any wobbles are opportunities for entrepreneurs who are poised and ready. This chapter asks you to consider the compelling opportunities that exist for your business in China, and whether your business might or might not be a good fit for exploiting China. It concludes with a reminder that change is the only constant, and that it is how you deal with it that defines how successful you will be.

WHY CHINA?

China is poised to dominate the global economy—more than any country ever has—as one of the most capitalistic and entrepreneurial nations in the world. Whilst President Donald Trump is ceding the global leadership mantle that the US had taken up since World War 2 with his "America First" policy, China has seized the opportunity to lead many initiatives, including climate change, renewable energy, and the globalisation of trade. China has the scale, work ethic, infrastructure, and control over its centralised economy to be incredibly successful and regain what it lost to the West during the Industrial Revolution of the 18th century. The nation's sustained growth is of a magnitude the world has rarely seen, achieving 8% annual growth in 2011, a year that saw the worst global financial crisis since the Great Depression of the 1930s, and continues to expand at an enviable 5-6% right now. There is the promise of even greater wealth on the horizon as China's domestic and international businesses mature.

China is set to become:
- Provider of Asia's regional and then the world's global currency.[1]
- Base of regional headquarters for all global businesses.[2,3]
- "Prolific developer of new technologies including biotech, fin-tech, robotics, environmental, and sustainable-energy technologies".[4]
- Best and fastest developer of new business, outpacing all other nations; it is already rated world number two.[5]
- Home to some of the largest and most strategically important cities.[6]
- Champion of domestically developed, homegrown global brands, helping it to become a leading consumer for all commodities

and jumpstarting the largest spending boom in history due to its expertise in mobile e-tailing.[7]
- Provider of one of the most important and the most widespread languages in the world.[8]

It's an exciting, awe-inspiring scenario. Add China's ability to change directions as needed, and you have a situation where you can do well if you are nimble on your feet, and have something to offer that is innovative and relevant. The specifics that make China my preferred area include the following.

Great Work Ethic

Work ethic is China's weapon. This nation of more than 1.3 billion people works with impressive intensity and quality. While wages are one factor, when you calculate the total cost of doing business, you cannot overlook work efficiency (productivity), which makes China the top choice as manufacturer and supplier to the rest of the world for the foreseeable future.

In China, getting workers to *stop* working is one of the biggest conundrums. Chinese factories, most prominently in the South, use itinerant labourers who live in dormitories at the factory. Each year, millions upon millions of Chinese from the countryside leave their homes to find work in the burgeoning assembly lines of Chinese cities. Their goal is to earn the most money in the shortest amount of time in order to return home and buy land, a house, or small business. Naturally, they seek out the factory that offers the maximum amount of overtime, which often means more than 100 hours a week. Spending leisure time in a shared dormitory isn't attractive.

The downside to this work ethic is balancing what the workers want (when it comes to hours) with what Western companies and the Chinese government labour laws require. Western companies write into their supplier contracts clauses about the number of hours each worker can be on the clock, while China's labour laws state that workers must be treated fairly with a rest day on the seventh day of work and a maximum of 60 hours worked in a week. If a factory boss stringently follows China labour laws and/or the rules set by their Western customers, and cuts hours and overtime, then his or her workers may quit and walk across the street to a competitor's factory that doesn't restrict hours.

When I took over the management of a lingerie factory with 2,000 workers in Guangdong, I faced a major problem: The factory was working excessive hours. The factory manager understood that this was a sticking point with the Western clients and explained that the only way to eliminate this was to implement two shifts, so no one set of workers worked beyond the legal 60 hours a week. The extra costs were affordable, so the second shift was approved. As a result, 40% of the workers quit within two weeks and went to work in a single-shift factory across the road where they could work upwards of 120 hours a week—a loud and clear message. We ended up going back to the original system. It's difficult to balance what the workers want with the rules and wishes of the Western brand, who is probably envisioning sweatshops without understanding the reality on the ground.

Getting Things Done
(Without Necessarily Understanding Why)

Chinese business owners and their workers have a can-do attitude that comes with energy and enthusiasm difficult to find in other parts of the world. The answer is very often, "Can," even to difficult demands. They commit first, and then figure out afterwards how to do it and deliver on schedule. I like this attitude, and have adopted it as my approach to business. However, the only hitch to this equation is that you must negotiate with common sense and realistic expectations, or you are guaranteed to be disappointed with what is delivered.

Problem-solving is also refreshing. In the West, it's very common in corporate culture to say, "I have a problem." Often, you simply report the problem because you aren't thinking about the good of the whole, or you might look at how other departments are underperforming and congratulate yourself. In China, it goes like this: "I have a problem and this is what we can do about it." It's more solution-oriented with less blame because it's in everyone's interest to fix the problem. Perhaps this comes from the Chinese agrarian background—a culture of practical solutions and getting things done. None of this means that things move seamlessly. You still must manage expectations with communication and training.

I was running a large trading company that had a sourcing office in Hong Kong, which is directly across the border from Shenzhen, China. I thought it made sense for us to downsize our Hong Kong office and open in Shenzhen because it would be cheaper to operate, with the added benefit of being closer to the factories. I challenged my China director to open a Shenzhen office in three months. Three months later to the day, I was invited to the office's grand opening with a traditional suckling pig ceremony. While my China director had followed the brief by opening in three months with 60 employees, I quickly realised that many of the so-called Shenzhen staff were in fact commuting from Hong Kong at higher cost. I assumed that he would understand my intent, but he simply fulfilled the brief in the easiest way possible. I should have clarified my expectations and defined what a successful outcome looked like. The physical office wasn't the goal; the goal was to cut costs and boost productivity by being closer to the factories.

A Dream Market

The Chinese market—home to more than 1.3 billion people with increasingly disposable incomes—has an amazing ability to both supply and consume all available products and services, which is an incredible opportunity for small-to-medium-sized companies looking to do business in China. In 2017, The Verge reported that Alibaba's Singles' Day sales amounted to USD25.3 billion, nearly double of 2016 Black Friday and Cyber Monday in the US combined.[9] Meanwhile, high-end sales in China are rising alongside the nation's wealth, increasing the demand for export-quality products at home. For example, wrinkle-free men's formal business shirts that cost about USD10 to manufacture, retail for the same price in Shanghai as they do in San Francisco. Sure, the percentage of people who can afford such shirts in China is lower than in the US, but when you consider the size of the population, the sales are meaningful.

For the past seven years, I have been on the management advisory board of a company making premium shirts and suits for the export market, including brands such as Calvin Klein, Hugo Boss, Zegna, and Banana Republic. Other than production, they had nothing to do with China seven years ago. Now, 40% of their business comes from domestic sales in China with the same margins or better than those from their Western clients.

Masters at Reinvention

The Chinese government actively implements growth initiatives, such as subsidies for state-owned enterprises and strategic industries. These are often put into effect quite abruptly. Nevertheless, whether it's a government initiative or a fluctuation in market conditions, China has an amazing ability to reinvent itself at lightning-quick speed as the market requires. It's your job to pay attention and stay ahead of these changes so that your business can move as necessary.

In 2009, for example, I started getting indications from factory owners that they were interested in doing business domestically rather than for export. At the same time, the Chinese government was in the process of switching its emphasis to driving growth through more reliable domestic consumption rather than exports, which had left the country overly exposed during a rough-and-tumble downturn of global economy. While Western economies were oscillating up and down, China kept its economy moving and growing through massive government-funded investments, such as infrastructure projects.

Part of the government's plan was to reduce the export subsidy for factories, via a rebate of value-added tax (VAT). Factory owners also told me that they preferred to sell domestically with RMB pricing as opposed to quoting export customers in US dollars because US dollar appreciation was significant. This allowed them to eliminate any currency-related risk.

Then, we went from a capacity shortage, principally led by a shortage of labour when export demand was high, to a glut of capacity and supply at factories, caused by a downturn in demand from the European Union and the US. In addition, customers in the garment industry began buying more styles in smaller quantities as Western retailers became more cautious and were eager to replicate the Zara business model of "fast fashion", even though it's far costlier to manage, because it costs the same to oversee the production of 1,000 shirts as that of 100,000.

Production over-capacity has been a boon for my business in recent years. Today, China still isn't producing to its full capacity. Sourcing products is much easier when the decrease in demand is coupled with a lower number of companies using China in their business plan when it isn't in fashion anymore, as Bangladesh became a better source for European customers because of duty free access to the EU. The factory owners on my current roster are eager to take on more business. They love to brag that they have plenty of work during their weekly mah-jong games, as it gives them face with their friends and colleagues who are typically struggling with over-capacity and not enough sales.

Keep in mind that with this reinvention, there is a strong need in China for creative input and technical innovations in products and services, along with efficiency gains from different systems of management, organisation, and engineering.

Something for Everyone in this Large, Sprawling Country

Thirty-four provincial-level administrative units make up China. Cities such as Beijing and Shanghai offer all the amenities and services that you'd find in major metropolises around the world. Head to China's interior, however, and you will find a China frozen in time with mostly agrarian communities with poor wages, little education, and ineffective infrastructure. This divide is expansive with sophistication and competitive business practices in the east, by the Yangtze and Pearl River deltas, and a west that is ripe for expansion. The rules and disciplines may not be in place in China's interior and smaller cities, but they will come. Western businesses working in China have played, and will continue to play, a part in that evolution, which is a win-win situation. Vast sums are being deployed in developing high-speed rail networks and new airports. I recently returned from Chengdu in western China, which now has a world-class, modern airport which puts to shame the run-down facilities of JFK and Heathrow.

WHAT IS IN THE FIVE-YEAR PLAN?

As detailed in "A Guide to Doing Business in China" by King & Wood Mallesons, the current Five-Year Plan of 2016 has just been refreshed and updated by President Xi Jinping at the October 2017

19th National Congress of the Communist Party of China (NCCPC).[10] It clearly identifies strategic opportunities and government-sponsored areas of growth and innovation. The areas listed below are perfectly poised for entrepreneurial expertise. If your skillset fits into one of these emerging industries, then you'll have no problem finding a way to make your business work in China, with the added possibility of financial and tax support.

Fintech and Financial Services

Asset Management
(Including Restructuring of Underperforming Assets)
There are already bankers on the ground in the marketplace, but they frequently don't know how to run the businesses they have invested in. This industry needs people who understand business operations, as well as the financial side. As part of my non-executive directorships, I gained experience with many underperforming assets in China.

Cash
China is being strangled by the Central Government's control of the banking sector. I have seen first-hand that top-down, heavy-handed commands from Beijing have starved thriving companies of cash. When one of my long-time suppliers suddenly tightens my long-standing credit terms without any apparent change in the business relationship, I know the banks have just turned the screws in response to a new Central Government directive.

A quick history: First, the government tried to address the enormous bad-debt ratios of its native banks by demanding that liquidity ratios be boosted. Then, the Central Government responded to the global economic crisis by decreasing the amount of loans given to businesses, knowing that a significant amount was going into property and share speculation. This resulted in a further squeeze on bank lending in an effort to suppress property speculation and the continuing problem of inflation. All of these policies resulted in companies struggling to get working capital, and coincided with a dramatic reduction in the cost of capital as US interest rates tumbled and Western firms factored RMB depreciation into their investment decisions. Bottom line: Chinese firms are all too eager to find partners with cash to inject.

Western Management Expertise

Creativity (New Product Development and/or Service Ideas)

New products are still the domain of foreigners. Akin to how the ancient Romans refined and capitalised on Greek inventiveness, China needs inspiration, and can run with it harder and faster than ever imagined. To date, few global Chinese brands have emerged, though many Western ones have been bought because of this trait. China needs creativity and product-development expertise to accelerate its evolution and competitive advantage. Significant recent purchases include Volvo (USD1.3 billion), G.E. Appliances (USD5.4 billion), Smithfield Foods (USD4.7 billion), Pirelli (USD7.6 billion), and AMC Theatres (USD2.7 billion).[11]

Manufacturing Sophistication (Moving Up the Value Chain)

China will continue to develop products and related technologies, while chasing new markets for these more sophisticated products and services. There is a lot of room to work with these manufacturers as true partners with your own staff in their facilities to help streamline their processes and advance to the next level of sophistication, whether with products or services.

Robotics may seem a luxury in a country with a workforce of over 800 million people, but there is a shortage of workers at every factory I use. The plentifulness of the workforce is a major consideration when factory owners select their factory's location; such is the difficulty in attracting workers to menial industrial production lines. Everyone aspires to a service sector job. This has made China a prime target for the introduction of simple robotics, which solves the labour problem and boosts quality of repetitive tasks at the same time. I oversee the production of 11 million pairs of swim goggles each year, and our main factories now dip the lenses in anti-fog coating by robot, resulting in a safer, faster, and more consistent workplace.

A recent Financial Times article by Michael Pooler[12] indicated that although from a low base, China was now accounting for over 25% of all industrial robots being purchased in 2016, which was a 27% increase on the previous year. Yet, I don't believe this figure captures the sheer scale of implementation, because the machines I see being installed are homemade, often in the mould-making or machine shop workshop by their own engineers. They are also from local companies who aren't registering on the Financial Times' radar. This approach actually helps China scale the value chain and retain its ability to supply its customers. It also assists in the trend towards smaller batches of a greater number of customised products.

Business Management Know-How
(Training Mid-Level and Executive Managers)

We all suffer from a shortage of strong mid-level and executive managers in China. The short history of privatisation and the growing employment market has created a drought of talent in the white collar and skilled-employee market. It also may be that the Chinese method of education, with its focus on rote learning, inhibits the ability to think independently and question orders received from the boss, in favour of loyal and blind following of orders. The opportunity to upgrade middle-tier management by having them work alongside experienced multicultural operators is a positive benefit for business owners wishing to upgrade their staff.

E-Commerce and the Sharing Economy

China leads the West in these areas. Whilst the inspiration undoubtedly came from Amazon, PayPal, Facebook, WhatsApp, and Uber, it is Alibaba, Tencent, WeChat, and Didi Chuxing which have perfected their business models and expanded at a rate that is unheard of. In many cases, the Chinese company is consuming its Western counterparts.

Alibaba aims to serve 2 billion customers by 2026 and employ 100 million people. They already enjoy 20 million reviews being posted a day, and their customers are interacting with them online for 3.4 billion minutes a day, virtually all from their mobile phones. The founder, Jack Ma, has laid out his goal: "Integrating online, offline, data and logistics across a single value chain."[13] When I buy breakfast outside my Shanghai office in Xu Jia Hui from the roadside *xiao long bao* (dumpling) stall, the vendor won't take cash, only Alipay, Alibaba's ubiquitous phone-based payment solution, though the cost is only RMB8 (about USD1). The cashless online future is already here in China, and all of the above Chinese companies have global ambitions, so in these areas it is better to come and learn than come and offer Western expertise.

China's Belt and Road Initiative

This initiative of President Xi Jinping has received both lavish praise and accusations of hype, so here's a summary of what I know from CBX Software's "Retail Sourcing Report" for 2017's fourth quarter.[14]

China's plan to create and connect vast sea and land routes across over 60 countries and three continents, known as the Belt and Road Initiative (BRI), has received considerable attention following a diplomatic forum in Beijing in May 2017 attended by leaders from 28 countries. Formerly known as One Belt, One Road (OBOR), the BRI consists of two components: an overland Silk Road Economic Belt connecting China with Central Asia, and an ocean-based Maritime Silk Road to China's south, shown in Figure 1.1. The plans include improving infrastructure and creating trade agreements with various countries. The China-led plan involves around 65 countries in Asia, Europe, the Middle East, and Africa, which make up over 70% of global population and is forecasted to cost around USD4 trillion.

Figure 1.1 Map of the two planned Land and Sea "Silk Roads" that make up the One Belt, One Road, now known as Belt and Road Initiative
(Source: 55 Consulting, adapted from CBX)

China stands to benefit most from this initiative, given that it will create jobs and expand markets and access to natural resources for China, as well as build extensive influence in regional and global affairs. It will also help to integrate and improve infrastructure and conditions for the remote regions of China. Many developing countries have responded well to the deal, given that it will provide necessary infrastructure to develop their own economies. One example is a China-funded railroad in Kenya, connecting Mombasa to Nairobi, which will eventually integrate African countries such as Uganda, Rwanda, and South Sudan.

However, some countries and organisations are concerned about the environmental, social, and financial risks of the BRI. Japan, Russia, and India are concerned about the geopolitical power and influence that China will have in the long term if the initiative is realised. So far, China has pledged over USD100 billion to finance projects such as the China-Pakistan corridor and a high-speed railway link connecting China and Singapore. China has also extended around USD900 billion in credit to countries such as Ethiopia, Kenya, and Sri Lanka, which is unlikely to ever be repaid. The United States is also clearly concerned about how this initiative will impact its own strategic and economic interests, and does not want China dominating the Eurasian region. President Trump was noticeably not present at the Beijing forum and has expressed clear intentions to push in favour of US versus global interests in all existing and proposed international agreements.

CREATION OF CHINA'S GREATER BAY AREA INITIATIVE[15]

For many years, Guandong, Hong Kong, and Macau were collectively tagged as the Pearl River Delta (or PRD).

Premier Li Keqiang announced in the annual government report in 2017 that the authorities were going ahead with a new, expanded initiative called the Greater Bay Area (GBA) initiative. The goal is ambitious: combining Hong Kong, Macau, and the cities of Guangdong's Pearl River Delta to create a region with an economic heft that is comparable to the San Francisco Bay Area, Greater New York, and the Greater Tokyo Area. To succeed, the relevant infrastructure, policies, and regulations will all have to be in place to ensure people, goods, and services are able to flow freely within the region.

Last year, the combined gross domestic product of the 11 cities in the area reached USD1.4 trillion, or 12 per cent of the national economy, even though it is home to only 5 per cent of the country's population.

They have a population of nearly 67 million, larger than the Tokyo Metropolitan Area with a population of 44 million.

It will build on the strengths of Hong Kong's financial and professional services sectors, Shenzhen's high-tech manufacturing and innovation skills, and the manufacturing strengths of Dongguan and Guangzhou.

The development of the area should also act as a catalyst for China's Belt and Road Initiative.

The development of the GBA is a key opportunity for Hong Kong. To take full advantage, Hong Kong needs to focus on three key areas:

- The sectors with the biggest competitive advantages: international finance, shipping and logistics, offshore RMB transactions, and dispute resolution.
- The unique features offered by the "one country, two systems", notably Hong Kong's adherence to the rule of law.
- The city's strength in combining its proximity to the GBA's manufacturing base with its connectivity to the rest of the world.

Free Trade Zones

The Free Trade Zones that have been piloted in Shanghai and Hangzhou are now to be spread to 13 zones, to stimulate provinces in the less developed areas. Tax rates will be set at 15% (normally 25%) and cross border e-commerce facilitated. Tianjin is specialising in creating an offshore financial market, whilst Xiamen and Fujian focus on trade with Taiwan.

Green Engineering

China has a target of manufacturing and selling 5 million new energy vehicles, and cutting pollution so that the particulate matter air quality indicator target falls from PM10 to PM2.5 by 2020. This is going to require Western expertise and possibly Western capital.

I'm personally expanding my own business to take advantage of some of these opportunities.

DOES CHINA NEED YOU?

What Makes You Relevant to China?

Your success depends on what you have to offer in a country that is increasingly savvy and sophisticated in both business and manufacturing. Today there is an army of 800,000 young Chinese attending universities, colleges, and schools overseas who will soon return to China with an international perspective, fluency in English, and knowledge of Western business practices. In 2008 there were just 180,000 overseas.[16] If you see your role as a bridge between Chinese factories and customers in the West, then consider yourself obsolete as factories now "go direct". Even if you speak Mandarin, it no longer carries the same weight if that's all you have to offer. That is the old model of doing business in China. The concept of an Old China Hand, a foreigner who had first-mover advantage with unique insight and connections, is a relic of the past.

The updated, relevant version is very different. Today it involves integration into the China-side business, not simply sitting in the middle taking orders and passing them to some China factory. A few years ago, I began to shift from teaching Western retailers how to negotiate with factories, to teaching Chinese factory management how to negotiate with Western retailers.

Look at what you can offer and explore if it's something that China needs. First, adopt the mentality of a China-preneur—find your niche and establish your relevance. Do you have experience and an in-depth understanding of the business sector you work in? Is it a sector that's in demand in China?

I have 30 years of sourcing expertise, not only on the operations and technical side, but also, to a lesser extent, on the sales and marketing front. This is an asset to my Chinese partners when it comes to adapting and building their business if they are lacking in these areas. I help them where I can to benefit their business, which helps boost my own business. It's the perfect symbiotic relationship.

Time Zone Over-Ride

Do you have a willingness to work whenever the customer wants to work—in their time zone? One of my biggest clients is based in the US city of Boston, which runs 13 hours behind Hong Kong in the winter. (Hong Kong follows Beijing's rule and doesn't employ an adjustment of clocks to account for the seasons). I am committed to spending my Tuesday evenings updating the CEO about the week's events, agreeing on priorities, progress, and problems. Every Friday, I reset priorities and solve problems with their Senior Vice President of Operations. In-between, there can be multiple calls each week depending upon need. I don't resent these evening calls—they are just a necessary requirement—and it allows me to read my kids a bedtime story before the US comes online.

Cultural Sensitivity

Face is supposedly an Asian-only concept that refers to the maintenance of one's dignity, honour, and prestige in front of others. In my experience, all races like to be treated well and not be humiliated in public. The Confucian concept of treating others as you yourself would wish to be treated is a safe rule when debating how to act. Of course, there are specific cultural aspects to face— for example how many minutes one must stay at a funeral to show appropriate respect, or how much money to give as a gift at a Chinese wedding, but there are formulae which locals know for guiding you through these processes.

Do you have the desire and ability to embrace the cultural divide to better understand your Chinese staff and partners? Often, what you see is not what you get. If you judge managers by a willingness to ask questions in meetings, you will be very disappointed in China. Getting opinions from your (or other people's) staff isn't a straightforward process because no one questions the boss—especially not in front of others. Comparisons with Western staff just aren't appropriate and must be put aside. Chinese schools have an average class size of 45 children. Rote learning is the key to memorising the three thousand basic Chinese characters necessary to read a newspaper—and to achieve exam success. This leaves little time to develop the ability to ask questions or be creative.

While Mandarin skills can go a long way to improving relations, I found that a willingness to understand the Chinese perspective is equally beneficial. Your relationships and your business will benefit tremendously from open-mindedness. I equated being gregarious, Westernised, and English-speaking with better performance, but the reality was that these employees were simply the best at dealing with the foreign boss rather than the best at doing their jobs—a key difference. Thankfully, a member of my staff was confident enough to point out my prejudices when she realised I was planning to give these staff the largest annual salary increases!

Entrepreneurial Innovation

China's rising class of innovators benefits from several built-in advantages:[17]
- The vast scale of China's market, which drives powerful efficiencies as new products and services are rolled out to hundreds of millions of people.

- Chinese consumers are enthusiastic adapters of new technologies.
- Entrepreneurs operate in a developing market unencumbered by legal infrastructure.
- China's shoppers quickly take to online shopping and digital payments, in part because they don't have to unlearn the habits of shopping in traditional brick-and-mortar stores. (With online sales this year expected to be USD1.1 trillion, McKinsey says China accounts for nearly half of global e-commerce worldwide.[18] Goldman Sachs expects a growth of 23% for the next four years, reaching USD1.7 trillion by 2020).[19]
- Chinese consumers' indifferent attitude toward privacy and antitrust rules enables Chinese tech giants to collect and analyse data—including where consumers live, where they travel, where they shop, what they buy, what music they like, whom they socialise with, and what kind of healthcare they receive. Chinese customers don't seem worried about the loss of privacy, as long as such personalised technologies make their lives more convenient.

Shenzhen is a city of more than 10 million people just across the border from Hong Kong. For those unfamiliar with geography and politics, Hong Kong became a part of China when it was handed back by its colonial owners the UK in 1997. Under the legally binding agreement signed to affect the transfer, Hong Kong became a Special Administrative Region of China, with separate laws and even separate passports guaranteed for 50 years (hence the phrase "one country, two systems"). So, crossing the border from Hong Kong to China still requires a passport or identity card and passing through two sets of customs and immigration officers. I live five minutes south of the border, and can see Shenzhen from my home. It is the high-tech hub of China, housing giant enterprises and thousands of start-ups.

Last year, I visited one manufacturer of Bluetooth earphones and speakers that employed 15,000 people. The founder had arrived in Shenzhen just five years ago with RMB500 (USD75) in his pocket. Now, he had an industrial conglomerate. The reason I was visiting was that he had decided that in order to expand his business, he would set up a business incubation unit. He already had many international blue-chip customers, and a superb 3D modelling and sampling capability. So, he was offering new start-ups a chance to partner with him on a 50:50 basis to develop their initial concepts and use his channels to market. He already had more than 100 entrepreneurs in his "crèche", and some of the initial ideas were dazzling. This was all from a guy who got on a train and turned up in Shenzhen to start a business.

What Works for Me

In China you'll find great attitudes, a lot of small and medium enterprises, and a concept of speed and flexibility that I've found nowhere else in the world. Amazing things can happen here and they can happen quickly. This is why China works for me.

I came to China under the pretext of making my business more relevant, but ended up discovering a new way of working and a country that truly wants to do business. Instead of Western apathy, jealousies of success, and difficulties in finding hard-working staff, I found a productive and educated workforce full of enthusiasm for making money and eager to learn from those who are successful.

The rise of China has created one of the fastest surges of wealth the world has known in the shortest period—albeit with extremely uneven distribution—and economic output is poised to continue on this path. The speed of development belies the patience required to achieve success in China. A lack of patience in the beginning can very easily derail your efforts if you aren't prepared for that frustration. But China is by no means slow, so adapt your current approach to business in favour of a nimbler one, and continually reengineer your business plan with a clear vision of how you can sustain it. It isn't about being a one-hit wonder, but continuously leveraging what you must to create the next opportunity, which is very often wrapped up in changes to the business landscape. You may not be the first to recognise them—I'm certainly not—but try to be early and proactive to stay relevant.

CHANGE IS THE ONLY CONSTANT

China continues to be one of the best bets for the future when it comes to doing business, but it isn't some magical land of Midas where everything turns to gold; and it also isn't immune to the usual laws of entrepreneurship: For every successful business, there are at least 10 failed ones behind it. If you aren't familiar with the culture and the rules of the land, China can be a country shrouded in mystery and myth, all fuelled by media reports that present partial realities of what's really happening. It's daunting, but don't be paralysed by the need for hard work or misleading headlines. The misperceptions suit me just fine. For those like me who have built careers on the rise of China, the current media-supported image of imminent doom-and-gloom helps eliminate fair-weather competitors from the pack.

Working in China is not for the lazy. Being quick on your feet is a requirement to keep up with the rapidly changing business landscape. Thrive on change and relish the chaos of it, all the while assuming that no business model is relevant for more than a few years. A business shouldn't be built to last, but rather, built to change. People, and the relationships you build, however, should be built to last. This might run counter to everything you know or were taught in business school, but innovation is a more interesting and business-saving option that offers quick action to accommodate market needs. Instead of saying circumstances have changed beyond your control, consider looking at the new possibilities that arise from a changed situation. Your next move is based solely on your attitude.

You will have small and huge issues thrown your way. Here are some of the peaks and troughs I've survived.

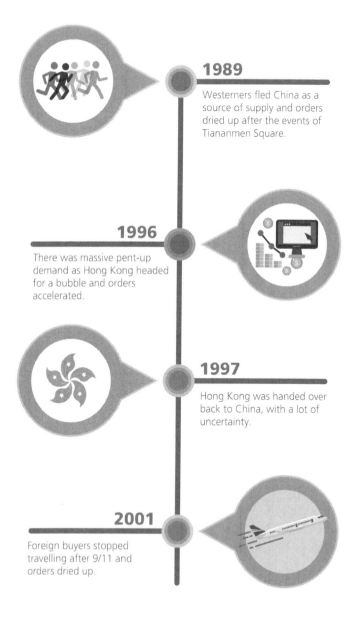

1989
Westerners fled China as a source of supply and orders dried up after the events of Tiananmen Square.

1996
There was massive pent-up demand as Hong Kong headed for a bubble and orders accelerated.

1997
Hong Kong was handed over back to China, with a lot of uncertainty.

2001
Foreign buyers stopped travelling after 9/11 and orders dried up.

INTRODUCTION: WHY CHINA?

2002

Dependence on China was a concern for Western retailers because of escalating tension in the Taiwan Straits. Suppliers in alternative countries were sought.

2003

SARS "bird flu" epidemic spread, curbing buyers' travelling and placing orders for six months.

2008

The global banking system experienced a meltdown, leading to erosion of confidence in the global economy. China orders were stopped and cancelled, which saw tens of thousands of China factories shut down.

2010

RMB appreciation became a serious concern, as did increases in labour costs when Beijing imposed a 21% increase per annum for the next three years. A lot of production shifted offshore to Bangladesh, Vietnam, and Cambodia.

2011

There was a shortage of workers and factories in China while commodity prices surged to record highs as China sourcing demand outstripped supply.

2012

China switched its focus to domestic demand as export orders withered. Too many export factories chased too few orders while commodity prices collapsed.

(2012)
Xi Jinping elected President. Various and largely ineffective anti-corruption agencies were centralised into one agency: the Central Commission for Discipline Inspection. Suddenly the traditional way of doing business and "greasing the wheels" changed. Over 100,000 people would be arrested within the next five years. Restaurants in China were suddenly empty, luxury watch sales plummeted, and fear was in every Chinese boardroom.

2014

Costs in China were still rising; factories were closing or reorganising, labour rates were moving closer to those in the West. Speed and innovation continued to be essential for survival.

2015

There was a sudden and shocking official devaluation of RMB on 10 August, due to extreme concern at loss of export jobs, leading to loss of confidence in stability.

2016

RMB continued a managed decline of close to 10% in a year against USD.

2017

Raw material prices (oil-based plastics and fabrics, cotton, paper, and packaging) escalated suddenly despite weak demand. RMB continued weakening as Beijing imposed more stringent restrictions on sending capital overseas and environmental pollution.

Despite rampant myths, China is still a smart place to do business with a base in Hong Kong. Here's a summary of the most popular myths and subsequent facts.

MYTH 1: With more than 1.3 billion people, China has unlimited labour.

FACT: China suffers from labour shortages when it comes to manual jobs. As counterintuitive as that seems in this huge nation, it's really supply-and-demand economics as usual. Migrants from the interior have more options for work. Factory managers prefer workers in their 30s and 40s, as they tend to stick to the job longer. Factories that have gone on strike have been able to do so because companies can't quickly replace the work force anymore.

But over the long-term, the supply of workers is still sufficient as people from interior China continue to migrate south and east in search of jobs. However, China is also suffering from a shrinking and ageing population, which prompted the elimination of the "one child" policy in October 2015.[20] This has yet to make an impact.

There is also a natural progression of workers wanting to leave manufacturing for more lucrative service jobs. The government is trying to improve this situation by dramatically increasing the minimum wage each year to create sufficient jobs at a sufficient wage level to absorb the unemployed.

INTRODUCTION: WHY CHINA? 27

MYTH 2
China is getting too expensive for production as it moves away from being the world's low-cost factory.

FACT
China's output cost can be competitive, because the increasing cost of labour can be offset by increasing productivity if labour as a percentage of the total cost is low. Raw materials will cost similar amounts whichever country you select.

MYTH 3
Factories in China can't sell directly to the West.

FACT
An agent can sometimes add value beyond translating and being a tour guide, but you have to look at your math and make sure it's justified.

Look at the mathematics of the garment business to give you a powerful incentive to go direct. A retailer buys a shirt for USD10 ex-factory price. If they use an agent to act on their behalf, the agent typically charges 6%. The retailer multiplies the ex-factory price by 4.5 to get the retail price in order to generate sufficient profit to pay for the supply chain, cost of capital, and import duties. It's straightforward that USD10 x 4.5 = USD45, which is the cost if a retailer goes direct, while USD10.60 x 4.5 = USD47.7, which is nearly an extra USD3!

This makes a factory suddenly appear to be 6% cheaper without having to do anything but bypassing the agent. They will sell more and make more profit if an agent is cut out of the equation. And many factory owners are sending their children to schools and colleges in the West. They return to China fluent in English and ready to do business with one foot firmly planted in China and the other in the West.

4

MYTH
Sweatshop conditions where staff are overworked and underpaid lead to major disruption, including suicides.

FACT
The workers themselves are leading the charge for more hours and will quit factories that follow labour laws and contractual stipulations from Western partners, for factories that offer more hours.

Suicide rates are actually three times higher in rural areas than in cities. 75% of all suicides occur in the countryside, according to statistics posted by the Chinese Centre for Disease Control and Prevention. Those that do occur in factory towns are perhaps a better indication of dreams dashed by young workers looking for management roles, apartments, or spouses.

5

MYTH
It's too late to start working with and in China.

FACT
It's never too late to start doing business with China, the largest exporter in the world and one of the fastest-growing domestic markets. There is plenty of growth to go.

Consider the current shift to a consumer-driven economy. This is happening right now and new business opportunities are emerging. The sooner you beat your path to China, the better poised you'll be to seize these chances as they arise.

RIDE THE DRAGON

With the right perspective, the constant changes in China are more exciting than threatening. It's stressful every time you must change things up, but the opportunities are also bigger. Assess the mood around you and reinvent your company and structure as needed. This might mean diversifying your portfolio to include different types of businesses or changing the structure or existence of an office. Either way, there are always new and more profitable opportunities that come from a perceived problem. Become the trusted advisor to both retailers and vendors who can help steer them through these rapids with frank and timely advice. Make specific predictions and build a track record of accuracy to demonstrate your added value. Seek out credible and sizeable financial institutions and trade information with them—they will value your perspective from the factory floor, and you will benefit from knowing their predictions concerning China before they become front-page news. Consulting businesses thrive on change—when everything is in "neutral" or "cruise control", potential clients have little motivation to seek improvement.

SUMMARY

- Bet your business future on a "rising tide". China is going to dominate Asia and then the world; now is the time to plan your role and exploit the opportunities.
- The combination of strong work ethic and "can do" attitude is compelling, and no amount of labour cost increases can deflect from this powerful combination.
- The government five-year plan clearly identifies where the biggest opportunities (and tax support) are; it is like a signpost to future success. The government desires to move up the value chain and move away from being the world's low-end producer of basic goods.
- Success and growth won't be linear; expect turbulent times and plan accordingly. If even Walmart can struggle, then success is not given, it has to be earned through your skilful navigation and understanding.
- Be brutally honest about your relevance to what China needs. Can you demonstrate how essential you are?

SECRET ONE: GENERATING TRUST

> "Never do to others what you would not like them to do to you."
>
> Confucius

Using Wes's experiences as a starting point, we start to understand the realities of forging trust-based relationships in China, and learn to read between the lines of the surface activity going on during any Chinese negotiation.

WES FLIES IN TO MAKE A DEAL

In a smoke-filled room in a remote factory in Eastern China, Wes, a jet-lagged and weary owner of a North American manufacturing company, stares across the table at his Chinese counterpart Mr. Chen, his supplier's chairman. Wes feels his blood begin to boil. He can't believe he's spent the last 24 hours traveling halfway around the world for this.

He stares at the people in the room and, in turn, places blame for his growing rage. He's angry with his Chinese staff, who, after months of haggling, couldn't close the deal. Now, at their request, he's sitting in this nicotine-stained conference room, all the while thinking, "Why can't they do their jobs? Why do I have to do everything for them?"

He's angry at the woman sitting across the table who awkwardly translates their conversation, giving the meeting the feel of a low-rent diplomatic mission as the presentation moves in halting fits and starts. "Clearly her English isn't that good. I know what I'm saying isn't being translated correctly. Why does it take her so long to say the same thing I'm saying?"

Mainly, he's angry with the man he's travelled so far to see. Wes was patient during the lengthy tour of the factory and listened respectfully through Mr. Chen's monologue at the start of the meeting, even though little of it seemed important to the deal at hand. He was tolerant of the deference everyone, including his own China staff, showed to Mr. Chen throughout the tour and meeting. But then, while Wes was presenting his pricing proposals, the chairman's mobile phone rang. Tired and frustrated, Wes waited for him to turn his phone off and apologise for the interruption. Instead, he took the call.

Shocked, Wes thinks, "The man I've travelled so far to see takes a phone call without apology in the middle of an important meeting? How can that not be an insult, in any culture or language?"

Before passing judgment, it would pay for Wes to consider Mr. Chen's perspective:

For months, Wes's company, a North American firm, has been going back and forth on fussy details for three small trial orders, taking up time and energy from Mr. Chen's staff. He tries to politely point this out—albeit indirectly—to Wes by talking in general at the beginning of their meeting about the number of customers and range of clients his company currently has, all the while painting the picture of a very busy operation with no shortage of work. "Surely now he will understand what he has been doing to us," the chairman thinks.

While Wes is thinking, "The hardest part is over. Now the real opportunity is here with a large-scale order built on the back of the test orders," the chairman is wondering, "They've been jerking me around, chopping and changing three small trial orders. What will future orders be like?" Instead of putting the chairman's fears to rest, what does this foreigner do? He launches into a PowerPoint presentation to try to squeeze the price down. This foreigner may be a busy man, but Mr. Chen is also busy with requests and demands from other clients around the world. How can this foreigner not see that he's wasting valuable time?

Just then the chairman's phone rings. On the line is a real customer, someone who has been placing bulk orders with the company for years. Without hesitation, Mr. Chen takes the call. And why not? A guaranteed order is worth more than the possibility of a bigger one that may come to nothing. They even have a phrase for this in the West: "A bird in hand is worth two in the bush."

In truth, the chairman does like what he's hearing about volume, but is worried about the fluctuation in prices of raw materials. "The orders are okay and what we hoped for, but how much of the raw-material price increases can I stick him for?" he thinks.

It's no wonder Mr. Chen's demeanour is reserved as the Western entrepreneur tries to win him over with facts and figures. How many similar presentations has he sat through before? The chairman looks at the clock in the room and wonders, "Why isn't this guy listening? I don't need him. Unless my margin is a solid 10%, there's no point in this deal. I'm not sure I can trust him." Still, the amount of business the Westerner is claiming sounds promising. The chairman clears his throat, and his words are translated: "It's getting late, and I'm sure you need some rest from your long journey. Why don't we pick this up later? Let me take you out to dinner this evening."

Although Wes would prefer a hot shower and room service, this company is the only choice he has until he lines up other vendors. His more seasoned colleagues have told him that dining together is an important part of doing business in China. He'll do the dinner to get Mr. Chen's backing in the short term while he considers his options. "Sure, that sounds great," he says. As he listens to the translation, he notices the tension in the room among the Chinese staff lifting.

Wes was smart enough to accept the dinner invitation—which was the only point of the entire first meeting. He didn't understand that this was the sole goal at the beginning of his meeting—or even at the end—but now that you know, act accordingly, and look for signals that a dinner is being considered.

The way China does business is not better or worse than the West. It's just different. Your aim should be towards merging the best of East and West, seeing the strength in both, and how they can complement each other. Let's consider how Wes could have prepared better.

LESSONS TO BE LEARNT

Nobody to Blame but You

Notice when the meeting goes awry, how Wes, our frustrated Western entrepreneur, begins pointing his finger in turn at the different players in the room: his staff, the translator, and even his would-be business partner. Noticeably missing from his growing ire is himself. You have to wonder if he even knows what's going on or how he's contributed to mounting frustrations in the room.

Trust Requires Travel

Wes did do one thing right. He got on a plane to China. Changing your mindset—that China isn't a short-term strategy, that it takes time to develop relationships, and that you can't start business meetings by going straight to the crucial issues, no matter how pressed you are for time—is no small task. Over the years, I have seen so many executives and entrepreneurs fly into China as the flavour of the month, only to beat a hasty retreat when times are difficult or a few failures mount up. Those who stay and persevere reap the rewards. They develop a bicultural acumen that matures as they continue to work in China with Chinese partners.

What's crucial here is to enter into the culture with a spirit of openness and non-judgmental interest. This is easier said than done. Every Western executive who steps into a Chinese boardroom would describe themselves that way, but thinking it and feeling it are two very separate things. No doubt Wes thinks he's a paragon of worldly thinking, even after flushing with anger as his potential business partner took a call in the middle of his meeting.

You now know that building trust requires both a commitment to travel to enable face-to-face meetings, and sufficient time to allow the relationship to form, via the dinner table to the negotiating table.

Set Realistic Goals for Meetings

After the fractious meeting, the Chinese staff in the room knew something that our Western friend had yet to realise. From the supplier's position, the point of the meeting wasn't to settle the pricing details of the contract. The true goal of the meeting? To be invited to dinner by the chairman where trust can start to be built. Food is incredibly important to China's culture, but also important to China's business culture. Eating in China is a favourite pastime. It doesn't matter if you've made great money together or if business is difficult, you can always "break bread" in a positive and productive way. It gives you the opportunity to get to know one another better and strengthens the foundation for future business. Wes, our Western executive, didn't understand that sharing a meal was his ticket to making things happen.

While the cuisine and teas varies from region to region, you'll benefit from paying attention. Once you understand which dishes you like, be sure to learn their names so you can suggest them when it's time to order, which is both impressive and flattering to your potential partners. Otherwise, you're going to be stuck eating the stereotypical foreigner meal of spring rolls, fried rice, and sweet and sour pork.

Understand Your Counterpart's Mentality

The chairman is throwing Wes a gracious lifeline. The deal is far from sealed, but Wes, despite his rocky audition, is granted entry to a place where relationships are built and fruitful business relationships blossom—the sumptuous dining halls and drinking establishments of China. Trust may or may not be enhanced over dinner. The location of the dinner and the entertainment afterwards will be key indicators of future commitments from the chairman. Played well, however, the result could be a stable business relationship lasting years; and this is where success can truly begin to take shape—for both partners. Try to remember that unless the deal is "win-win", the loser of the two parties will pull the plug rather than continue. As I expand on later, contracts in China are meaningless if they have to be referred to.

Guidelines on Relationship Building

I've talked a lot about trust and how it's key in any relationship, never more so than when money and your livelihood are at stake. But how do you build it? When you first head out to meet people in China, here are some rules to keep in mind.

Dos:

- ✓ Invest face time. Potential China partners like to deal with the owner because that person makes the decisions and pays the bills.
- ✓ Always pay on time. Never forget that trust building is done with money. If you can't pay on time, advise them in advance with a damn good reason. Your partners need to be assured at all times. The mantra is, "*No surprises.*"
- ✓ Put your own people in their factory. This is an extension of the previous point. It's one thing to help train them, but it's another to give them an expert focused on their business and on site on your tab.

(continued)

- ✓ Take leaps of faith with advances and prepayments (while understanding that it might be a gamble you'll sometimes lose). You have to take the lead with this and be the first one to put money down.
- ✓ Consider paying a bit earlier before Chinese New Year. This gesture can go a long way. Factories have to pay their workforces their annual bonus, and cash is always tight. Demonstrating your understanding of this, even with a token prepayment, will demonstrate your understanding and trustworthiness.
- ✓ Share know-how and market requirements with the factory. They will see this as an investment on your part.
- ✓ Share about your business *and* your life. You're selling your company and they're selling theirs. You're interviewing each other. It helps to have a current PowerPoint presentation ready on your computer or tablet, with details about your business, customers, and targets; include videos showing your product being used, and on display at major retailers and websites. This helps avoid a lot of misunderstanding.
- ✓ Establish mutual fairness. It has to be win-win for both parties. You can't be the only one making money. Sometimes the business will be better for them than for you, and that's OK.
- ✓ Think long-term. Introduce factory owners to your customers. If you've established mutual fairness, then you shouldn't have to worry about your customers going direct with factories. If you've built trust and everyone is happy with the profit at the end of the day, then that brings loyalty to the mix.

(continued)

- ✓ Sign a non-circumvention/non-disclosure agreement in Chinese and English. You're going to be sharing information, customers, products, and designs. This isn't a negative; it's a positive.
- ✓ Last, but not least: Always be punctual. Aside from lateness implying you value your time as more important than your counterpart's, it also infers your orders might be inconsistent or delivered late.

Don'ts:

- ✗ Order your shipments as late as possible, forcing your suppliers to run raw material inventories without firm orders, in order to accommodate these last-minute scenarios.
- ✗ Constantly change orders.
- ✗ Raise quality complaints without having a plan to fix them. Sometimes complaints are justified, but they're frequently used as justification for getting out of orders and/or getting the price down.
- ✗ Be difficult to work with. If you are, then you're a long way off from building a lasting relationship.

However, there are certain things you should note.

Relationship versus Contract

There is a stark difference between the legal cultures of China and North America. In the West, contracts are legally binding. In China, they are treated more like a "memorandum of understanding", while *guanxi*, or the personal relationships you've built, trump any laws or written agreements. The rule-of-law culture, whilst strong in Hong Kong, is still in its infancy in China. This puts even more emphasis on building trust while doing business in China. I tell all my clients, "If you ever have to consult a contract, it means the deal has gone bad and you should terminate it." Until you completely grasp this truth, don't bother negotiating a deal in China.

Managing Expectations

The world moves fast, and speed is a competitive advantage, but the faster you go, the more mistakes you make. Setting expectations is a continual job, and establishing clear standards can't be skimped when you work in China. Never assume anything is understood until nailed down.

Setting standards, providing training if needed, and physically being present will not only save you a lot of headaches, but go a long way to show your new partners that you're invested in them and your shared business. As with any venture, you must be prepared to put in the time, which might come in the form of sharing your expertise to help move your partner toward development and away from a "copy" mode. The Chinese are masters at lightening-speed production, but in order to achieve amazing quality to your specifications, you must be present, make reasonable demands, and make no assumptions. Otherwise, you leave yourself open to major disappointment.

At the end of the day, the Chinese are as serious about building a business and making money as you are, and they think long-term. If your gut instinct tells you that they have what it takes to build that kind of relationship, then do what you can to reassure them that long-term is the direction you're aiming to go. You want to sell the prospect of working together and continuously negotiating, and not necessarily just prices. Target areas that might need tweaking may include quality or lead times, so shine a light on them as you begin to work together. Think of it as negotiating via a progress report. The start of a project is the most difficult time because your new partners aren't sure how much business you'll give them down the road.

YOUR WORD IS YOUR BOND

It sounds simple, but if you approach every meeting in China on the basis that you expect to be cheated, you probably will be! That's because you may be projecting your hostility and suspicions upon the other party, and starting with a defensive posture. Instead, try demonstrating your confidence in the potential of the *partnership* by exhibiting trust in the joint business plan. Inject a tangible demonstration that you are a fair operator. Perhaps raise the issue of payment terms before the factory does, and suggest that a 50% deposit for the first order (to cover the raw material and packaging costs) is reasonable, providing that when orders start building your normal trade terms of "TT 30 days after shipment" is available. Or ask if you could bring your US customer to their facility for a site visit once production is underway. This demonstrates you are secure in your relationship with your end customer and not afraid of being bypassed, and is generally perceived as a demonstration of confidence and longer-term partnership.

SUMMARY

- Treat people as you'd like to be treated.
- Establishing trust requires travel. FaceTime, Skype, and other forms of videoconferencing are not substitutes.
- Target to get, and then immediately accept, the offer of a meal together!
- Don't rush in demanding to finalise a deal—establish a relationship first.
- Set realistic expectations upfront in order to minimise surprises. Understand the goal of every meeting from both parties' perspectives. Relationships are two-way streets—sell your company and partnership potential rather than assume everyone wants to do business with you.
- Mutual fairness is an essential component of any long-term deal. If something is too good to be true, it probably is. Use common sense.
- It isn't possible to teach trust—but hopefully you now see the way in which you can engineer the best opportunities to build it. That's how I've developed my own "brand" which begins with integrity and trustworthiness.

SECRET TWO: MASTERING NEGOTIATION

> "Teachers open the door,
> but you go through it yourself."
>
> Chinese proverb

This chapter starts with Wes's fictional example of a difficult negotiation with Ann, a Mainland factory owner. It covers many typical bargaining challenges, and then explores some simple guidelines that I've developed over the last 20 years to improve your chances of a successful outcome.

WES PLAYS "GOOD COP/BAD COP"

Wes is preparing for one of his forays into China, because his Shanghai and Hong Kong staff have failed to get the deal he demands from his largest supplier Modern Mouldings in Yi Wu. Wes likes to use classic "good cop/bad cop" role-playing when he has a complicated pricing deal. Wes plays the "voice of reason", trying to bridge the gap between the factory owner's expectations and what the "bad cop" (his manager) is demanding. He has a clearly defined goal but understands there are multiple ways of getting there. Identifying the leverage "items" he has is critical.

Knowing only too well the incessant delays caused by Shanghai air traffic control, which affect almost every single Hong Kong to Shanghai flight, he is happy just to arrive before the day is more than halfway over.

The problem is a little daunting. Wes ordered USD8 million worth of products from Modern Mouldings in 2017, but was hit with delays just as peak production was due to ship (just before Chinese New Year, when factories shut for three weeks). Wes's team found that the factories were subcontracting much of the production to small third-party factories very late in the day. Instead of reporting the problem and asking for help, the owner had lied, reporting that weekly production targets were being met on time, and when the large pre-Chinese New Year shipment became due, she faked a fire in the corner of her warehouse and claimed it had destroyed much of the stock.

For the balance of the season's shipments, Wes has held back a USD1.5 million buffer from the payments owed to her because of the likely chargebacks for late delivery that he would be receiving from his US customer. He hadn't yet allocated the orders for next year and was waiting to reach agreement with the factory on how much they would contribute to the fines he would receive. The factory owner was anxious to get the cash she was owed, and the orders for next year, yet wanted to pay just a nominal sum towards Wes's chargebacks.

In fact, Wes was keen to retain using the factory for 2018 because their pricing was so competitive and they had a large amount of machinery which was unique to them—competitors had to outsource part of their production, whereas this factory, if they chose, could do everything in-house.

The battle lines were drawn and Wes had just a morning to meet with the owner to achieve a satisfactory outcome. He wasn't sure whether to blame his senior manager for failing to negotiate a reasonable outcome, or be impressed that she had called him and said she couldn't make a deal on her own and needed his help.

Wes had already met with his Chinese senior manager Helen (who was responsible for dealing with this factory) a week earlier, when they had agreed upon the "zone of success" that they would try and achieve. She had conducted more than 20 phone calls during the week with the owner, listening to all her excuses and the rationale of her argument, finally getting her to offer USD300,000 cash if Wes would immediately return the USD1.5 million cash.

Now Wes felt he knew what was important to the boss of Modern Mouldings—she was willing to settle for a larger cash sum, but only if the payments could be staged over several years so she could get immediate return of the money she was owed. And she was hungry for orders for next year.

Before the meeting, Wes and his senior manager played out several different scenarios—altering the amount of fine and the terms of settlement (when to pay), in effect creating "sliders" to adjust the pain to each party, to see where a fair middle ground might be, and to establish his bottom line. The fine had to be sufficiently punitive to cover the immediate costs that Wes would owe the retailers, but not so much as to bankrupt the factory.

Even before the meeting started, Wes gained a helpful assist—the vendor was driving to Shanghai from a distant city and was caught up in traffic, and would be 30 minutes late. This gave him a psychological advantage, as he had flown up especially for this meeting, and was sitting patiently waiting for her to arrive.

Ann, the owner, and her sales manager started the meeting by explaining that oil prices were rising, and to expect price increases by August. She added that in the 15 years of running her company she had never been asked for chargebacks. Wes explained through his Chinese manager that the customer had asked for a major contribution due to late deliveries, and he had no choice but to comply if he wished to preserve his relationship with them. And similarly, she had no choice but to contribute to his costs if she wanted to maintain her relationship, and recoup her USD1.5 million. Wes explained that the USD1 million claim excluded all the time and travel he had invested in flying managers from both Hong Kong, Shanghai, and Boston to her factory to try and help rectify her loss of control over production at her subcontractors.

Ann balked at the USD1 million figure, and explained that she had always supported Wes's company, only made a 2% net profit, and had swallowed the in-season PVC price increase from RMB8,500 to over RMB10,000 per kilogram. Wes accepted that she had supported his company, and that the USD1 million chargeback figure could probably be shared between both parties. Ann replied that the most she could offer was USD200,000. Wes replied that whilst he appreciated her position, he couldn't shoulder the burden of such an enormous chargeback.

At this point, on prearranged cue, Wes's manager Helen went crazy, shouting at Ann and highlighting the appalling way she had handled the late shipments, and the derisory amount she was offering as compensation—Wes had asked for USD1 million, so offering USD200,000 wasn't even worth discussing. Wes reinforced the point that if they couldn't agree, it was best to give up and let the lawyers proceed, and although reluctant to do so, Wes would have to retain her USD1.5 million until the court ruled, and she wouldn't get any business for next year.

This led to a ping-pong exchange of USD50,000 increments, eventually leading to an offer of USD450,000 now and USD250,000 over the next year. But with a stinger—only if Wes would guarantee a minimum of USD6 million business for the next year.

This was the opening he needed; Wes accepted the USD450,000 plus USD250,000 paid in a year's time, and promised to call immediately to release USD1.05 million of the USD1.5 million he had owed her. He carefully explained that he could not guarantee a future turnover, because demand was uncertain, and how competitive would Ann be in future years? He could offer to make his "best effort" every year to maximise his business with her company by allowing her to see the final pricing from all competitors, and let her match the lowest price to secure the programme. At this offer Ann conceded, and everyone shook hands. Wes had his manager write out the agreement in Chinese, and each party signed both copies.

All negotiations have similarities whatever the ethnicity of your opposite number. It always pays to be prepared, know the impact of constituent ingredients, and consider multiple scenarios. But bargaining with Chinese vendors requires a different perspective. As Tony Fang puts it in *Chinese Business Negotiating Style*, "Chinese do business with you, not with your company."[1] It's personal; corporate entities are made up of individuals, and decision-makers are expected to take personal responsibility for carrying out their promises. Hiding behind corporate decisions is not advisable and unlikely to be tolerated. The same applies to the head of your supplier; your deal is with him. Make sure he knows you will hold him personally accountable. Don't be fobbed off with other directors or managers.

Now, let's consider how you can achieve similar success in your negotiations.

LESSONS TO BE LEARNT

Life is a negotiation, so it makes sense to master the basics, whether you are trying to get your kids to put their shoes on and go to school, or agree with your partner on what movie to watch. It takes the same skill set as negotiating cost prices with Chinese suppliers, just a different perspective and stage.

I've taught over 1,000 senior managers in London, Hong Kong, New York, Los Angeles, Shanghai, and Dongguan the basics of negotiating between Western brand owners and Asian manufacturers. My introductory joke is always the same: A man goes into a shop and asks to buy a tin of baked beans. The shopkeeper says, "That'll be $3."

"$3!" says the customer. "That's a crazy price. It's only $2 in the shop next door."

"Well, then go and buy it next door," replies the shopkeeper.

"I can't," says the customer. "They've sold out."

Anyone can submit a quote on anything, and the new party will typically undercut the incumbent supplier. But sourcing *effectively* requires *pre-qualifying* those invited to quote to ensure they have the capability to deliver an identical product. Typically this will require the supplier making a sample and auditing their production facilities. In other words, a cheap price from someone who can't sell you what they claim they can is worthless.

Planning

The whole meeting took over three hours, but Wes's preparation paid off, and his manager played her part well. The outcome was positive, and business can move forward. Wes was careful not to overplay his hand and be too aggressive; the factory owner could have taken the refund and run away, refusing to do his orders for next year if she felt he wasn't being sufficiently balanced. That's where experience comes in. The reason Wes got a good outcome was because he adhered to the following guidelines.

Before the Meeting:
- Understand the cultural background of the other party.
- Have a "zone of acceptable outcomes" in your mind, not just one fixed goal.
- Absorb the fact of life that if a factory owner can't make 10% profit on your order, why would he or she take the risk of doing it? And would she still be in business to complete the order?
- Ensure the meeting is with the company owner or CEO; don't be fobbed off with sales managers and directors. Only one person calls the shots and can make decisions.
- Find out exactly who else will be there, and match their headcount with your own staff, if possible.

In the Meeting:
- Start with pleasantries.
- Sell your company. Have a PowerPoint with videos summarising why you are the best choice. Focus not just on existing customers and growth potential, but also financial stability. To paraphrase, ask not what your opposite number can do for you, but what you can do for them.
- For a first meeting (as we saw in the Trust chapter), the goal is just to be invited to dinner. Do not underestimate its importance and do not decline any hospitality offered, irrespective of jet lag!
- Do not rush to the main point of cost prices; there is a "dance" to be conducted before reaching this stage.

- Asking costs nothing, but be clear what you offer and expect in return.
- Interruptions are the norm in China; it's not personal, just a different code of conduct. Shrug them off and don't let them impact your equanimity.

Many Factors Impact Pricing

It is vital that you understand that the overriding factor in setting a price for a product *isn't just its cost to make*, or the margin both buyer and seller wish to make; it is the status of supply and demand. What factors should you consider when negotiating the price of a product with a Chinese manufacturer? You might be surprised to learn that the actual cost is only one element (and not necessarily the dominant one).

Supply and Demand

Four times a year I provide my clients with a forecast to provide guidance as to how they should negotiate. Specifically, my clients want to confirm the bottom-line increases or decreases that they should agree to pay. The following is a list of the key factors, in order of importance, to help you plan:

- Retailer demand. This is the overriding factor. When demand is weak, factories will charge less; when strong, they'll charge more.
- Availability of bank-borrowing facilities. This is a major concern in China, where capped lending by the government to control inflation has led to a black market for loans with interest rates that start around 18%.
- RMB outlook. Depreciation or appreciation makes an impression on the final cost when customers work in US dollars, as do the factories in China. As of early 2018, there is no sign of this abating,

and the medium-term prognosis is for the RMB to further weaken to 6.7, as shown in Figure 3.1.

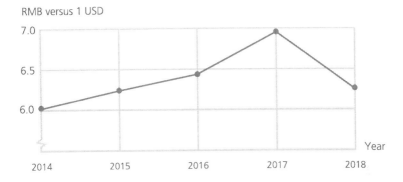

Figure 3.1 Fluctuation of RMB versus USD from 2014 to 2018 (on 1 January each year)[2]

- Labour costs. The Central Government confirmed another 14% to 21% rise in minimum wages, with more in the south to entice more migrant workers, and less in the north.
- Inflation (especially of utilities). The real rate is currently close to 10%.
- Raw material pricing. Cotton, for example, has been highly volatile. It became part of many hedge-fund portfolios as prices doubled.
- Better sourcing of trims and labels. (Forcing your suppliers to use components that can only come from a single approved source inevitably worsens your prices).
- Offshore competition from Vietnam and Indonesia. This competition suppresses China's pricing power.
- Factory rationalisation. The trick is to use fewer factories to improve how important you are—with more leverage—to those remaining factories.

I've worked through years where we were short of factory capacity and chasing to place firm orders and sign contracts to prevent being outbid by competitors. Then there are years like right now, where there is a shortage of orders, and this trumps all other rises in costs, because hungry factories offer the lowest prices.

But to be balanced, this equally applies to labour within China. Right now, annual increases are slowing down from their previously high 20%+ p/a increments. But that doesn't help when our factory owners have trouble attracting workers to our very basic industry. As with most industrialising nations, workers in China aspire to service jobs. If they must work on a production line they favour electronics, which is cleaner and better paid.

When things change, we give our clients advanced warning of how the cycle is going and how to respond. Typically, that means placing more orders as supply dries up or fewer orders as supply becomes plentiful and the advantage for pricing shifts to the retailer instead of the factory. Pricing power determines the profit that the factory and retailer can make on any order.

Payment Terms/Financing

The terms you negotiate say a lot about the relationship you are building, and the leverage each side believes it has. Some buying agencies leverage their relatively cheap cost of borrowing (at the time of writing around 2% p/a in Hong Kong for USD loans) with the negative cash flow experienced by their customers. In effect, they are using financing as a lure to secure their business. Aside from these middlemen, you need to understand the traditional financial instruments used and the common payment terms factories offer. Traditionally, overseas buyers offered letters of credit (LCs) which were "factorable", i.e., banks would happily take them as collateral to provide lines of credit. However, the cost of these LCs became unreasonable. Banks exploited their complexity and charged a "correction fee" for every error (missing punctuation or misspelling) and given these were overseas companies contracting Chinese vendors with complicated names and addresses, these "correction fees" quickly escalated. So, American buyers demanded that they pay by TT (originally named after Telegraphic Transfer, but nowadays meaning Electronic Transfer). The art of negotiating decides what terms these TTs will be paid in. The span is anything from 100% deposit upfront before any work is conducted (which is of course most untrusting of the factory but may be applicable where the parties don't know each other), to payment 120 days after shipment (most punitive to the factory but beneficial to the buyer).

Let's explore the hidden implications of the usual terms in the Chinese factory marketplace. Paying a 50% deposit upfront is reasonable if each party is new to the other. After all, raw materials need to be purchased so this gives the factory a reassurance that the orders are real. But ensure you get agreement that this *only* applies to the first order. Subsequent orders should move on to the industry standard, which is TT + 30 days. There are customers with cash flow problems that try for TT + 45 days or TT + 60 days to boost their cash flow. Remember, nothing in life is free, and factories will build in the increased interest costs and possibly take out insurance (if their bank deems you a credit-worthy customer). Beware of factories willing to entertain even longer terms of TT + 90 days or even TT + 120 days. These demonstrate desperation and should be avoided. They may dump your order when a better one comes along, or not be in business for much longer.

Reliability

Reliability is obviously a critical negotiating point and part of the cost price of any product—a cheap price without on-time delivery or correct quality, or even the financial stability to stay in business, is unattractive. There is inevitably a trade-off between reliability and price; you have to find the optimum formula for your business.

Attitude

The attitude of the owner counts a lot—flexibility and willingness to discuss the inevitable changes that take place once a selling season starts are valuable assets.

Interpret the initial quotes you receive. Benchmark them against at least two other factories. Get signed quotations on "chopped" (stamped) letter-headings to try and eliminate "ghost quotations" where unscrupulous staff manufacture quotes to make their favoured vendor the standout option. If you receive an unusually high quote, don't be disappointed; typically it is the factory not wishing to reject your order by saying, "No", so they offer an uncompetitive price in the hope that it puts you off! It's then time to find out *why* they don't want to work with you.

How You Sell Your Company to the Factory

This isn't a one-way trade. The vendor can make your goods to your designs, but you have to demonstrate you have products that are innovative and desirable, plus channels to market. Who are your customers? What is the size of your turnover? Why are you a better bet than your competitors? What is your growth track record in the last three years? Have you a website with videos demonstrating your products being used? How long has your company been in existence, and how long have you had a presence in Asia? Who are your bankers in Asia? All these factors will influence both the vendor's willingness to work with you and the premium they will charge you.

Ease of Doing Business

If you and your team are late in confirming orders, or make last minute changes, or are constantly decreasing quantities, or failing to meet agreed minimum order quantities per style, this will impact the price. This is frequently called "the buggeration factor" and factories charge their clients for their ineptitude. This can run as high as a 10% loading, and is one of the easier costs to suppress, providing you understand the critical path involved in taking your products to market. Having an annual time and action (TNA) calendar and sticking to the milestones is critical if you want to minimise not just delays but the inevitable frustrations and increased costs of doing business for your vendors. It's just like hiring a contractor to carry out a major home improvement project. Have a detailed plan of the works, agree on a costing and a timeline, and stand back and let him or her complete the work, as you keep a close eye on the timeline versus the progress. A clear plan which is adhered to will always stand a higher chance of being correctly executed.

I understand that in today's fast-moving retail environment, requirements change and no one wants to continue making goods that won't sell just because there is a plan to do so. But my mission is to eradicate all the inefficiencies caused by disorganisation and lack of discipline. For example, why design products without considering the need for packaging (especially for boxed goods or those sold in plastic clamshells or sleeves) and artwork at the same time? Typically, companies focus on developing product, and then at the end, rush to meet the dates that the artwork and specifications of the packaging are needed. This is just inefficient, and causes bottlenecks.

The first year, a vendor might be surprised by your lateness, failure to "freeze" decisions at agreed milestones, and by your indecisiveness about what you want. But you can be sure that in the second year, he will have factored into his costings a buffer for such mishandling. My estimate, obviously variable from client to client, is that there is an up-charge included in the costings, of 10% for those clients who cannot get their act together. Coordinating your product development, sampling, quality assurance, merchandising, and shipping departments to adhere to the previously agreed timeline isn't easy, but the price of failure is needing too many people to overcome the lateness of decisions, and a fractured relationship with the vendors. Right now, we are in an oversupply situation in China, but I have known long periods when demand outstripped supply, and I was begging factories to make my products. Then, suppliers didn't just consider price and margin when picking and choosing which orders they would make, they considered loyalty and longevity, and ease of doing business.

Bill of Material

The bill of material is the breakdown of components in a costing. If a factory owner can't make 10% profit on your order, why would he take the risk of doing it? But it is also true that you don't want him to earn any more than he has to in order for him to be motivated and complete the contract.

I use a simple table with all my clients that assesses the key elements in a bill of material, and ensures all merchandisers are familiar with what to expect. Table 3.1 represents a generic USD10 product. It highlights major components and their costs for a typical consumer product. FOB refers to the cost of goods "at the factory gate" and delivered to the container port—Free On Board—and is the usual way prices are negotiated.

Cost Components	Average Percentage of FOB Cost	Average Component Cost	Expected Percentage of Change	Expected Cost Impact	Remarks
Labour	20%	$2.00	10%	$0.20	Increase of labour cost by 10%
Material	65%	$6.50	10%	$0.65	Increase of material cost by 10%
Packaging	10%	$1.00	20%	$0.20	Shortage situation. Increase of packaging cost by 20%.
Transportation	5%	$0.50	0%	$0	Oil-based component. Factory to port delivery.
Total	**100%**	**$10.00**		**$1.05**	**Price of product impacted by +10.5%**
Impact of currency exchange rate (USD/RMB)			-4%	-$0.20	Assume only 50% of cost components are impacted by the currency exchange rate. USD/RMB exchange rate was 6.25 last year but assume 6.5 now.
Impact of price reduction			-5%	-$0.50	Drop in global demand for this product. Price softens by 5%.
Overall Price Impact				**$0.35**	**Overall, price of product impacted by +3.5%**

Table 3.1 Chart highlighting major components and their costs (Source: 55 Consulting)

Table 3.1 challenges you to know the impact of each element on the total cost price, and provides guidance on the various key components. It helps you ensure you factor in the major elements that go into a product's cost price, and anticipate what targets to set your merchandising teams in the next round of negotiations. It professionalises the "gut feel" many people have in the sourcing industry by insisting on a weighted approach to known factors, and by helping to manage expectations before each season.

Of course, each industry (and product within it) is unique, but price trends for all of them are easily found on the Internet, and can be verified by meeting with many vendors. This example recognises the rising raw materials, but factors in reduced demand and weakening currency, meaning that merchandisers should expect to achieve prices no more than 3.5% higher than last year.

Naturally, you must beware of "asking a barber whether you need a haircut"! Many clients regularly challenge me about currency predictions, or raw material prices. The factories tell them that labour costs are surging, raw material prices are far above last year, and demand is strong, whilst the RMB is plateauing rather than further weakening. The smart negotiator armed with this chart will seek third-party verification.

Coping with fluctuations and rising costs takes some foresight and shuffling. Much is written about the scary increases in labour costs within China, and it's hard to disregard, especially as 2012 was yet another year of between 14% to 21% increases, in addition to rising government social-welfare costs that each employer must bear. The flip side is that a significant part of those rises is mitigated by China's ability to continuously improve productivity.

Speed to Market/Minimum Order Quantities

This is having an increasing influence on the cost of products. Thirty years ago, when I trained as a buyer at Marks & Spencer, we only bought for two seasons a year. We had to guess more than a year ahead what the customer would want to buy. Fast forward to 2018, and Zara and the Internet have altered the speed at which trends are adopted and discarded. E-tailers such as Amazon, now registering its own fashion brands, and ASOS are challenging traditional retailers, despite the limitations of not being able to try on the product and assess the quality and fit.

Fast fashion has resulted in the entire fashion industry buying far more styles in far less depth (quantity of each), in order to assess which are successful—then the race is on to repeat the success by making a lot more of those styles in as short a time as possible. Or cancelling plans for any more if unsuccessful. Either way, I have witnessed a significant decline in the line planning and framework buyers prepare to assemble their offer—instead there is more of a "spray and pray" mentality, where vast numbers of designs are created and tested, to identify the winners.

It is much more desirable to minimise stockholding of unsaleable products, and limit the endless markdowns that old-fashioned department stores still adopt to this day (called high/low, where customers are assumed to be dim-witted enough to think "50% off" the initial ridiculously high price is a bargain worth snapping up). But at what cost are these changes being made? It costs a buying office (whether the giant Li and Fung with up to USD20 billion shipments a year, or a small 10-man office owned by a brand) virtually the same amount to create and ship a product whether it is for 1,000 pieces or 500,000 pieces. Obviously, the cost is amortised over very different quantities. So, the "race for greater options in less initial quantities" is sincerely needed by retailers, but the cost of servicing these increasingly complex orders is uneconomic for those organising the production, as well as for the factories, who inevitably prefer longer "runs" of product without changes. This is the tension faced every day between economies of scale and online consumer-driven requirements.

The solution to this new problem is, ironically, to go back to the skillsets we learnt to handle the booming mail-order catalogue business of my youth. In the 1970's through to the 90's, companies printed giant colour catalogues at great expense, and we arranged a small quantity of goods to be produced of every style, and only once the brochures hit the doorsteps of customers and demand became concrete did we produce in bulk. This required a unique niche industry, dominated by Taiwan in those days, that had:

- Pools of common fabrics that can go into multiple styles.
- "Prepared for dye" clothes sewn together, but dyed *afterwards* to improve responsiveness.
- Smaller factories with multi-skilled workers who could deal with a variety of machines and techniques.

There was a premium to pay for this, but its benefits outweighed the costs of producing giant quantities in the hope that the consumer would buy them. The Internet has simply reinvented the catalogue that was sent to your home. The acceleration of mobile purchases indicates the importance of impulse buys of people on the move, but the principles to service it are tried and tested.

KNOW YOUR DESTINATION

The old army saying, "Proper Planning Prevents Poor Performance", applies equally when bargaining with Chinese suppliers. Understanding the components of a negotiation, practising the arguments, and demonstrating leverage are all stepping stones to securing an optimal outcome.

The trend is for customer/supplier relationships to move from an "adversarial" model to a "partnership" approach. Each party must demonstrate why it is the preferred partner of choice—and should be treated as such. There may be a glut of factories at the present time, but there is a chronic shortage of excellent vendors with great attitude.

Speed and flexibility are becoming as important as cost—and require negotiating up front.

SUMMARY

- It's personal. Any deal is between you and your supplier's boss, not your companies.
- Be prepared. Work out scenarios that may occur before the bargaining begins, and how to exploit them. Define your goal or "zone of success".
- Understand the multiple constituents in a cost price. It's not just components and labour that impact, but also the current state of supply and demand, payment terms, reliability, attitude of both parties, bill of material/component costs, and minimum order quantities and speed to market. Are you aware of them all, and can you demonstrate how they make you a preferred customer?

03
SECRET THREE: NETWORKING WITH PURPOSE

> *Heaven helps those who help themselves.*
>
> Chinese proverb

This chapter starts with the example of how Wes leverages his contacts to complete a seemingly impossible order. We then look at where to network, defined as "socialising for professional and personal gain", reviewing and assessing the multiple sources available that you can use.

WES CONNECTS

One Saturday morning, Wes is relaxing in his hotel, the Kowloon Shangri-la in Tsim Sha Tsui, just across the street from his Hong Kong office. He didn't really feel like he was in China when staying there—it was an oasis of Westernised civilisation—and he tried to stay in Hong Kong whenever possible, leaving his staff to go into deepest China to visit factories if possible. He is in the coffee shop enjoying a rather too extensive breakfast buffet, which didn't sit well on top of his jet lag. The dining room was crowded, and Wes contemplated how 20 years ago, this hotel was full of American buyers. Nowadays, most of the customers were Mainland Chinese families, who didn't seem to understand the etiquette of queuing to help themselves to food, especially when the seafood and sushi counter was replenished, when hordes of people would strip bare the offering in minutes. Still, Wes was at peace with the world; the staff knew him and offered to get him anything he needed so he didn't have to contend with the crowd, and he was anticipating with glee his usual Saturday morning ritual of immersing himself in reading about the New England Patriots' next game.

Suddenly, Wes received a phone call on his new iPhone X. It was from an old contact, the CEO of a large US customer, for a rush order of denim that could make everyone involved a lot of money if he could pull it off. "I can get an order for 300,000 pairs of jeans if you can produce them in two weeks," this CEO said, adding, "The company desperately needs this sale. Make it happen!" Wes quickly went to work back in his room on his phone, and gathered favours from various vendors and fabric mills. After a relentless day of sourcing fabric, trims, labels, and production capacity, one of his largest Dongguan vendors not only committed to making it happen, but also bought all the fabric and ordered extra staff that very morning based on mutual trust and history. For Wes's part, he committed to being on site to oversee the quality control inspectors during the final inspection so they were commercial, and not too zealous. He became involved in every aspect of this deal because he couldn't afford to make a mistake. The factory understood that Wes was sharing his expectations and would be involved in making it work out with as few hiccups as possible.

The order shipped on time, everyone was happy, and Wes is still working with the same factory. They may not always be the cheapest, but they trust each other and know that when things inevitably go wrong, they can work together to correct it. This fabulously profitable order was done on a virtual handshake with not a contract in sight.

LESSONS TO BE LEARNT

As we saw with Wes, it is only trusted networks that can allow you to short-circuit the formalities usually associated with turning initial product concepts into delivered orders, and achieve the speed necessary to make the impossible possible.

Networking is like going to the gym—it's important for your business, but you must make a conscious effort to do it consistently. The good news is that you can do it any time of the day, every day. The easiest way to get started is to join chambers of commerce, but in a city like Hong Kong you'll also meet people socially. In fact, you'll find that connections will often come fast and furious because people are here to work and make money. Once you begin to build your network, try to find a delicate balance between fostering your relationships and not spreading yourself too thin. Some people in your network will serve as mentors and friends while others could be potential partners. Don't underestimate the power of your network and how much it can help you.

For example, I had a scenario where one of my clients was interested in working with a large toy company in China, but wanted to check it out first to see if the factory had integrity. The company structure wasn't straightforward, with different layers of businesses, so my client was understandably apprehensive about moving forward. I didn't personally know this company, but through my network and a few phone calls, I was able to get an accurate assessment of the vendor in a few hours—the calibre of senior management, staff numbers, and their financial situation. With this detailed information in hand, my client felt confident enough to make the decision to proceed with this factory—an example of how your network can add value for your clients and put you in greater standing.

Creating Your Network

Here is my take on the building blocks available to create your effective network.

Chambers of Commerce

Chambers of commerce are an easy starting point. As well as each major country having its own, there are powerful umbrella ones such as the European Chamber of Commerce and the Hong Kong General Chamber of Commerce. Annual dues are modest and regular events are hosted to aid networking as well as learning about relevant issues. I've been at various times a member of multiple chambers and attended specific events as a guest where interests overlapped.

I've participated in the British, American, and Hong Kong Chambers of Commerce at various times, but their non-industry specific nature didn't make them an ideal fit for my needs. They are more for initial integration into Hong Kong than hard-core business generation.

Business Forums

Business forums are a wonderful resource and learning platform, and the source of many of my closest friends, clients, and mentors, as well as providing my own board. These include local chapters of global networks such as the Lions Club Rotary, Young Presidents Organisation, and industry specific ones such as the Hong Kong Trade Development Council (HKTDC), and Hong Kong Productivity Council. These all require sponsors who propose prospective members, and each has his or her individual criteria and goals. They are worth investigating as each has clear websites that give an insight into what they can do for you, and what they expect you can do for them and the community.

I owe much of my success to the support and stimulation I have received upon joining the Young Presidents' Organisation (YPO). YPO is a global platform for chief executives to engage, learn, and grow. Members harness the knowledge, influence, and trust of influential business leaders to inspire business, personal, family, and community impact. It has more than 24,000 members in 130 countries, diversified among industries and types of businesses. YPO has been responsible for:

- Supporting my determination to leave corporate life and run my own company.
- Providing my own personal board who critique all my ventures.
- Generating multiple invitations to become a non-executive director.
- Supplying my mentors.
- Facilitating my ongoing education.

These types of forums are typically by invitation only, and it was only after my initial contract was up in Hong Kong and I had decided to make it my home that I was open to developing closer ties with Hong Kong businessmen and women. It's probably not your starting point but useful to foster.

Industry Forums

Industry forums are a useful way to meet your peers. I joined a Kurt Salmon Consulting roundtable breakfast meeting that met once a month, inviting all the heads of Western Retailers Buying Offices. I got to meet and know my opposite numbers at Macy's, Sears, VF Corporation, Target, and Karstadt, to name just a few. Firm and useful friendships developed.

The consultants got instant feedback on their topics and a great database to draw upon, whilst the participants could benchmark their own plans against their competitors. Topics were specified each month—it might be currency forecasting one month, or the expansion of sourcing from China to Cambodia and Vietnam, or the "risk/reward" of producing in Bangladesh versus India. At the time, I was managing Calvin Klein sourcing and it allowed me to be more knowledgeable in the eyes of my CEO because my strategy was based on the knowledge of what other major brands were doing.

An example of where it helped concerns social compliance auditing, the requirement to have a third-party audit at every factory a label uses, to ensure the brand's specified "code of conduct" in relation to child labour, overtime, labour law, working conditions, and safety, are being correctly implemented. China has one of the strictest labour laws in the world—unfortunately it is rarely implemented. (For more on this, see Secret 6).

One day, I was having lunch with the head of Polo Ralph Lauren sourcing when he got a call from his personal assistant to say that his largest and best factory had just failed a compliance audit. He asked to have the report emailed to him because he didn't believe it, and indeed the third-party audit company had found several violations, all relating to fire escapes being locked. As this factory was also being used by Calvin Klein, I wondered if we had received an audit too. My personal assistant confirmed we had, and sent it over. It was identical, with the same failings. But each of us had paid USD1,300 for the report. The third-party audit company hadn't just ripped us off by selling the same report to both of us, it had deliberately exaggerated failings because that way, they would have to go back to retest in a month, and could earn a second set of USD1,300 fees from multiple brands.

One excellent by-product of this was it inspired me to stop using unreliable and dubiously motivated third-party audit firms, and to set up my own independent social compliance auditing firm. It still works today for a host of industry names such as Adidas, PVH Corp., and others, and stands alone from most auditors because it only reports the truth and doesn't seek to generate extra fees by multi-selling or failing reasonable factories.

Industry forums are by invitation only, but if you are operating a sizeable business then the "host" may be interested in adding you to their stable of members. It's an excellent way to meet peers, and competitors. I would recommend it. Search online for suitable hosts.

Conferences

Conferences can be a goldmine of contacts, but are usually less useful when it comes to the actual presentations. Truthfully, I find most of them of limited interest. But over the years, I have learnt that there is *no* correlation between how much I expect to enjoy a conference, and how useful and interesting it turns out to be. I really try to stay open-minded about what I go to and when, sometimes choosing because the location is conducive to either work appointments or leisure breaks, sometimes because of the people I hope to meet.

Because most conferences are generally charging to make a profit, I naturally prefer attending when I am invited to speak. I attended a National Retail Conference in EPCOT/Disney Florida, and discovered I'd be sharing the stage with Walmart's head of sourcing. He flew in minutes before we were due to present, so I'd no idea what he'd be saying, and vice versa. It turned out we completely contradicted each other about how best to manage Asian sourcing, but this provided the audience with plenty of contrasting views, and was the start of my long-term relationship with Walmart, which I am still working with today.

My long-term interest in social compliance (the code of conduct Western retailers create to enforce their rules regarding the treatment and safety of workers in their nominated factories) led me to attend a conference on this subject hosted by the Chinese Government Ministry of Textiles. In the lobby I met Professor Denny, who was lecturing at Peking University International Law Faculty, and this led to a fascinating series of lectures, which he asked me to co-present with him. He explained the theory, and I explained the practical implementation of labour law in China from Western brands' perspective. We were then invited to Shanghai where the Communist Party has a training facility for city mayors, and asked to give a lecture on what criteria Western companies use to assess where to locate factories, and how best to unify the Western and Chinese interpretation of their labour laws. This opportunity not only led to friendship and a great deal of learning on my part, but also greatly increased the authority and credibility that I could speak with to prospective clients.

On another occasion, I was invited by a major client, the CEO of Hudson Bay Department Stores, to join him in attending an international convention of department stores in Beirut, purely because he wanted to recommend my company to his peers in other countries. This very generous gesture led to a very long-term relationship with the innovative CEO of Edcon Group, the biggest retailer at the time in South Africa. I ended up helping them to terminate their buying agency agreement and set up their own sizeable office in Shanghai.

Hong Kong hosts multiple trade shows and conferences, and I have found it best to attend several a year just to keep up with industry trends and meet one's peers. I try and attend the Asian Retail Congress conference each year. I would recommend this as a good starting point to broaden your network.

Continuous Education

I have been greatly influenced by a one-week YPO course at London Business School a few years ago with a group of 100 CEOs from around the world. This course was "case model" based. We were given examples of a specific company's problems along with budgets and balance sheets, and divided up into study groups to analyse and then present back to the entire group our recommendations. Typically in such courses, these results are then debated with the professor and compared to what subsequently happened in real life. But the genius of this course was that after the first case study, in which every group criticised the CEO and had multiple suggestions for how they would have done a better job, Professor John Mullins introduced a man at the back of the lecture theatre who was the actual CEO! He then proceeded to spend several hours debating with us about what he had done and why. This opportunity for real life interaction with the company founder was fantastic. We were working on real-life issues with access to the CEOs of each case study, and the CEO got input from 100 peers on his potential plans!

The biggest benefit of the course was from the small five-person study groups that we were put into. I was able to become closely acquainted with the CEOs of a wide variety of businesses—Middle Eastern colleges, Canadian telecoms, Romanian real estate, and a UK temporary worker agency. Two of these subsequently proved invaluable when I joined the board of a Chinese investment fund that was investing in colleges and telecoms. I had an instant sounding board that enabled me to better assess the viability of the businesses that were candidates for investment.

Ongoing education can be seen as a luxury, but if treated as an investment rather than a cost, can be highly beneficial. I remember having to present my business plan to five strangers and justify my strategy.

It was very beneficial. Although there are networking opportunities, so many people come from varied industries that it can be interesting rather than compelling to attend in your early days in China.

Non-Executive Directorships

Non-Executive Directorships (INEDs) are my passport to both networking with purpose and gaining insights into other businesses. Although typically modestly paid, the learning available in exchange for your experience makes this the best way to expand your knowledge, network, and skillsets. The knowledge you have of your own industry is typically based on sound, generally applicable principles you have learnt over time, and which can be applied to multiple sectors. Because they value the discipline and systematic approach I was trained to operate under, I have advised a chain of cafes, a short-term letting business, a manufacturer of remote controls and Bluetooth devices, and many other disparate industries. In return, you will learn many new facets and ways of running businesses, as well as be able to network purposefully with your fellow board members. Many of mine have become my advisors, partners, or friends.

All companies with aspirations for growth and strong corporate governance need a diverse board of directors. If you have an accountancy background and are a certified public accountant, you may be prized as head of the audit committee. Or if you are a lawyer, you may be recruited to handle legal matters. As in my situation, if you are just a generalist, your recruitment may depend on your general experience. Boards generally recruit specific skillsets for certain committees—Risk & Audit, Remuneration, and Nomination. (These three committees are mandatory in the UK under the UK Corporate Governance Code for public companies).

Before reviewing the specifics, it is my experience that there is a significant difference between public and private companies. I've been a director and chairman of both types, and inevitably the onus and responsibility is significantly greater with a publicly listed company. However, in Hong Kong we also have a hybrid—the family business where the owner/founder sells part of the business through IPO, yet retains a minority or majority stake, and adopts a board to meet the official requirements. There are examples where the owner still feels he is "in charge" and not accountable to the board or the shareholders. In these cases, the board may be filled with family and friends, and expected to rubber-stamp the owner's decisions. Naturally, these are best avoided.

Private companies are an excellent introduction to being a board member. Typically, after a successful consulting contract I would be invited to join the board. In many cases this was "continuing to get consulting but on the cheap". But it served as my apprenticeship and I am grateful to have been given these opportunities. I have served on the board of multiple types of businesses, including as chairman of a private tech start-up, as chairman of a London-listed China investment fund, and as non-executive director of a private plastic injection moulding company, where I helped with its complex sale to a competitor. I have also enjoyed five years of working on the board of a Hong Kong-listed electronics company. A key learning for me was that sound principles and streamlined processes are at the heart of any business, irrespective of market sector. For example, my experience in outsourcing was as pertinent to the electronics company as it was to my own business.

Of course, being based in Hong Kong led to my frequently being the only Westerner on a board. Stereotyped as being blunter than my Chinese colleagues, this also was used by them when difficult news had to be imparted. I recall being nominated by the CEO to introduce to the very traditional Chinese chairwoman of the plastics company just why we should diversify into making adult sex toys!

INEDs are the single best educational opportunity available, but it is a result of networking effectively in the other areas mentioned above, so it is not of initial focus.

Advisory Boards

Advisory boards are another starting point for networking with purpose and broadening one's portfolio—without any legal responsibilities. These groups of experts are designed to assist and challenge the CEO's thinking. I've been on many such boards and always learnt a great deal about how other businesses operate, and about best practices in other companies, which you can benchmark against your own.

My very first appointment, as I looked to broaden my education whilst CEO of a Hong Kong-listed trading company, was from Polo Ralph Lauren Sourcing, a Singapore-based company that controlled all of Ralph Lauren's global sourcing. My experience managing Calvin Klein's global sourcing was what they wanted to tap into, and my board was enthusiastic about me taking it on because of the opportunities it might yield. I got involved in several areas, from buying back licenses to expanding the sourcing base into Africa.

I also spent seven years on the advisory board of a major garment manufacturing company in Southern China. This allowed me to see the "other side of the table", and involved a broad range of activities, from monthly management reviews to attending annual management retreats with 200 managers in bizarre Chinese resorts, where company strategy was laid out in Mao-style five-year plans which no one questioned and everyone wrote down wordlessly.

How best to get started? In my experience asking others if they'd be prepared to sit on your own advisory board (assuming you respect their potential contribution) is a great way to start. Such positions may or may not be compensated. Typically, smaller companies just pay expenses. However, all offers should be judged against what educational, rather than economic, value they will offer you. The first position is always the hardest to get—once you have a position, it is much easier to access additional ones. This leads to a warning: *do not* overload and accept more than you can handle. I did—at one point being on seven boards at the same time—and it simply isn't worth the time commitment and organisational skills required to stay on top of so many part-time appointments. Bear in mind that it's not just the quarterly or monthly meetings—competent CEOs will want to meet prior to each meeting, as well as seek advice from you in between, and circulate tons of documents to wade through.

Similarly to INEDs, sitting on advisory boards is a result of networking effectively in the other areas mentioned above, so it is also not of initial focus.

Professional Network

The professionals we all need to run a business, such as lawyers and accountants, are a great source of networking. They may introduce you to other clients of theirs in similar fields, or sit on boards that need additional directors. Hong Kong is perhaps slightly unusual in that it is so commerce-orientated that if your lawyer thinks you are competent, they might ask to invest in your business, or introduce you to businesses that they have invested in that could benefit from your expertise. Both happen to me frequently whilst I am discussing my legal needs.

There are two points I'd like to make whilst discussing lawyers:

- I have one lawyer whom I specifically call my "contract lawyer" because I prefer a range of lawyers that I feel comfortable using for specific specialties, such as property transactions, intellectual property and trademark registrations, employment issues, and shareholder agreements.
- Manage your lawyer; don't expect them to manage your case. Just as with doctors, where it is your health at stake, you can't delegate the decision-making involved. Lawyers are paid by the hour, so aren't incentivised to find quick solutions or outcomes. And poor ones never give a recommended course of action. Those that start with, "On the one hand...." aren't being helpful! I found my specialists

all through personal recommendations, and in the best cases they become trusted advisors whom I go to for strategic insight and pay for the execution of legal documents.

Your professional network is a great place to start. Don't be shy, get personal recommendations for lawyers and accountants, arrange meetings, and ask for help networking.

Invitations

Seize opportunities by accepting invitations. I was once invited to attend a CEO round table dinner by our IPO advisor. By good fortune, the chief economist of a major bank was present. After getting to know each other, he confessed that his commercial colleagues were keen to do business with my public company, and wondered how they could get a chance to work with us in the future. I replied that we were always open for business discussions, but right now I had a poor impression of his bank because they had just rescinded the terms of a personal mortgage they had offered me, and it had left me high and dry. He apologised on behalf of the bank and we agreed to have lunch a month later. Next morning at 9am, the head of mortgages came to my office, personally apologised, and agreed to honour the terms of the offer letter.

Suppliers

Finally, your suppliers are a resource. One of my consulting clients hired us to gather commercial information regarding what brand leaders in the US were planning on buying for the next season, and how to expand their vendor base to be more cost competitive. There's no need to travel to Paris to see future fashion trends. All you do is ask several good vendors in China what samples they're making and for which brands. By partnering with two strong woven (denim) and knit (polo and T-shirt) manufacturers, I could offer the highest quality market intelligence.

My reputation was enhanced, the factories got a new customer, and my customer got access to US market information six months in advance. (Of course, being liberal with whom factories show their product development work to is a benefit if you are seeking market intelligence, but a major concern if it is your designs that are being shown to your competitors. Secret 6 will tackle this topic).

There are the obvious opportunities for industry knowledge sharing amongst your suppliers. Remember, as Wes found out in the Negotiating chapter, most business in Asia is done over breakfast, lunch, or dinner meetings. There is no shortcut for accepting this hospitality. Being invited is a compliment—treat it as such. You never know where it will lead! My motto has always been: "Never too busy to have a cup of coffee with anyone." Hong Kong is one of the best places in the world to network. Everyone is constantly working and looking for opportunities.

This is literally free—both in terms of access and time invested. You are already working with these suppliers—why not expand your discussions to seek their assistance? When I was running Calvin Klein sourcing, it was a common supplier who introduced me to my opposite number at Ralph Lauren, leading to mutually beneficial information sharing and ultimately my joining the Polo management advisory board.

Guanxi—What Is It?

China has become more modern, but you still have to take the time to build face and *guanxi*, which focuses on relationships and connections. Loyalty grows through this process, whether it's with your staff or customers. The principle is to say, "Yes," when you can, and offer your time and expertise when it comes to training. If you have people in your debt, then you have favours in the bank. You'll be thankful for your credit in this loyalty bank when you need to call on someone to help. This is particularly true with factories. I suggest building a core group of factories, a secondary group that typically works with you for three to five years, then as needed you can pick up freelancers by project.

Think of *guanxi* as "brownie points" from and to your network. Do whatever you can to accrue favours: give advice, meet for breakfast, or help existing customers outside of your responsibilities (by finding a technician, for example). Strongly believe in giving in order to receive. Down the road, you'll find that people have a good memory and you'll be able to call in those favours when you need help, and people are usually willing to help if they can. This is the main driver for how I operate. Don't go into this considering what's in it for you, though, because there's no way to know.

When I worked for Warnaco, it suffered a major blow to their US business due to audit problems. This resulted in the US parent company filing for Chapter 11 bankruptcy, which gave it the ability to walk away from any pre-existing contracts. Even though the Asian operation was profitable, this put me in a very awkward position when all the suppliers were due to ship and weren't certain of being paid. I renegotiated the terms and the flow of goods, all the while understanding there was a strong possibility that they might stop supplying us. The thing that saved me in the end: the factory bosses had known me for more than 10 years, and trusted me. I gave them my word that as soon as I heard of *any* problems I would call them personally, otherwise I wouldn't let them down, and they trusted that. I managed to keep 49 out of 50 factories operating at full speed, which allowed the company to come back out of bankruptcy within two years.

As another example, I have a relationship manager at my bank in Hong Kong. It's her job to help me, and in return she infrequently calls to try and sell some financial products to me. I'm always respectful and courteous, but I seldom partake in what she has to offer. There came a time when one of my major customers had a problem paying a check in from overseas. I went to see my relationship manager and she resolved it in a fraction of the time and with much less stress than it would have required otherwise. I put in the time to build a relationship with her and she helped me out when I needed it. You never know when and how someone can help. And besides, why wouldn't you be courteous? It just makes sense.

NETWORK "NARROW AND DEEP"

Go out and seize opportunities and accept invitations. Select just a few of the many networking opportunities I've listed above so you aren't stretched too thin at the start, overcommitting and unable due to time constraints to fulfil your obligations.

Good luck, and feel free to reach out to me if I can be of any help, at steve@55c.biz.

SUMMARY

- Seek out a variety of rich seams of potential clients, because the harder you network, the luckier you will get.
- Draw upon and develop all of your contacts, using: chambers of commerce, business and industry forums, conferences, continuous education, non-executive directorships, management advisory boards, lawyers and accountants, invitations, and suppliers.
- Be available, and try not to pre-judge what is and isn't worth your time.
- Build your own "bank" of favours owed—otherwise known as *guanxi*.

04
SECRET FOUR: BUILDING YOUR PLATFORM

> A gem cannot be polished without friction,
> nor man without trials.
>
> Confucius

Now, we get into the specifics of setting up in Hong Kong as a base for your China business. We start by learning why Wes decided to open offices in Hong Kong and Shanghai. Then we work through the lessons to be learnt from my own many mis-steps, including the advantages and challenges of setting up in Hong Kong, and go through a "to-do list" to get you started. Finally, we look at the realities of feng shui.

WES DECIDES TO SET UP HIS OWN OFFICE

"It's like that scene in Star Wars where all the aliens from different planets are drinking together in a bar," Wes thought. He was enjoying his usual pre-dinner beer in Lan Kwai Fong, the expatriate bar district adjacent to Hong Kong's financial centre. It felt as if everyone had come from somewhere else and was going somewhere else. From what he could overhear, the customers seemed to be discussing doing business all over Mainland China, but transacting it through Hong Kong.

Wes was waiting for Julie, the merchandise manager who looked after his account at the buying agency he was using, to proposition her. Rather than pay 6% commission to the agent, he wanted to do what his competitors were doing and set up his own operation. He thought it must be possible to do it cheaper that way. He had big plans to grow from USD120 million in sales to USD200 million p/a in the next three years, and there was no way he wanted to pay a middleman 6% of USD200 million. He could just hire Julie, add a few staff, and rent an office! But even more importantly, he felt Julie could get better prices if she was working for him rather than for the agency; he just knew the buying agency was choosing factories based on their preferences rather than what was best for his business.

Julie turned up on time dressed in a black suit with a knee length skirt, looking slightly uncomfortable and frumpy in the noisy bar. She knew that the chance to jump from being a merchandise manager to a general manager would take another 10 years at her company, if ever, and she was impatient to be promoted. She knew what Wes was going to ask her to do—she just wanted to make sure he was serious and understood what was involved… and what she wanted out of it.

Wes suggested they move to a nearby Italian restaurant called Va Bene that was quieter and more discreet, and there began outlining his plan. To Julie's surprise, it only took 10 minutes. She thought he would have outlined to her a business plan with costs, timelines, banking credit arrangements, and accounting services already planned out. Instead, Wes just had a vague plan to "do it himself" with her help.

Julie wasn't yet prepared to share with Wes the way her current employer operated, but she knew they were focused on maximising turnover rather than getting Wes the best prices, and that the factories selected had to pay the agency for various services, such as using their IT systems, insurance, and providing credit at peak times of the year, which they often complained about. So, she was 100% confident she could improve Wes's sourcing right from the start.

Julie began peppering Wes with questions: How many staff should she plan for? What was her budget? What size office did Wes want and where? Who was their bank and how much was he putting into the account? Would there also be an office in Dongguan and Shanghai, or just in Hong Kong? Did she need to hire an accountant? Would Wes keep an office permanently in Hong Kong, or one day shut it and relocate to the Mainland? (This was one of Julie's primary fears as she didn't want to work across the border. Many companies were relocating, and at the age of 37 she still lived at home with her elderly parents and didn't want to move away from Hong Kong).

Wes leaned back and looked across his empty plate. He didn't know whether to be impressed with Julie's questioning, or annoyed that the whole process of setting up his own office and dealing direct with his suppliers was more complicated than he had expected. Clearly, there was a lot of planning and some key decisions to make before he could start, but was Julie up to the task? Wes began to realise that he was going to have to rely on her for everything, from managing his money to signing contracts in Chinese that he couldn't understand. How well did he really know her? They had travelled to suppliers together every four months for a couple of years, and she was clearly smart and spoke fluent English and Mandarin as well as her native Cantonese, but was she trustworthy, and was she going to be loyal?

* * *

Two years later, Wes was once again sat with Julie in Va Bene, eating the same veal Milanese, but this time toasting the success of their Hong Kong office. It had been harder than either had expected, but the benefits had been larger and he felt in control of sourcing now, rather than reliant on middlemen. Julie had become his right hand, but there was still much to do to improve the calibre of the staff.

LESSONS TO BE LEARNT

Wes decided *what* to do—open his own office—but this is the relatively easy part. Far harder is *how* to do it. We will be exploring the factors you should consider, what you don't know, where to begin, and the differences (pros and cons) between choosing Hong Kong versus Mainland China as your entry point.

Are Hong Kong and Mainland China Really So Different?

Hong Kong is a city made for doing business, especially with China. The simplicity of setting up a business and running it, with the help of government transparency, low taxes, and the relative ease of hiring qualified and trustworthy people (compared with China) makes the Hong Kong Special Administrative Region of China (SAR) an excellent base if your business is related to China. In addition to a vibrant lifestyle, there is also an amazing networking element to Hong Kong. Think of it as a hub with spokes that can lead to numerous opportunities throughout the region. You can, of course, set up your base in China, but it's a lot more complicated and risky, with the rules constantly changing, and it is more difficult to navigate. Taxes are negotiated rather than fixed.

Back in my factory management days, I ran a 2,000-worker unit in Panyu, China, about an hour's ferry ride up the Pearl River Delta from Hong Kong. As an American-owned corporation, we diligently paid all specified taxes each year. I was summoned at the start of the next tax year to play golf with the mayor. The cause was the amount of tax we were paying. He pointed out that it was embarrassing that our relatively small lingerie factory was paying more tax than any other foreign company in his domain, including giant blue-chip tech companies. He asked me to reconsider and offer a fairer amount for next year. I had great trouble explaining to corporate headquarters in New York that the Panyu mayor's office was requesting we pay less tax, and was prepared to issue a letter confirming that we had complied with the national law!

Transferring money to and from China is something else that is a craft rather than a science. Regulations change frequently, and the banking system in China is very different than that of Hong Kong. I learnt early on that Chinese loan facilities were available but at much higher interest rates than in Hong Kong (because the Hong Kong dollar is pegged to the US dollar and therefore follows US interest rates).

And the system in China requires the full repayment of the loan at the end of its tenure. Only then does the credit committee, headed by the bank's general manager, consider your request for renewal. So even with his prior blessing, it may still take two weeks to several months to renew the facility—and there have been times when the Beijing central government suddenly instituted severe credit restrictions which meant no new loans, leaving at risk thousands of business that suddenly run out of cash. This has led to the rise of an entire industry of "grey" bridging loans at very high interest rates of 20+% per year. I was caught out several times and had to pay unacceptably high interest rates whilst waiting for my loan to be renewed, despite having the bank's confirmation that it was a formality. It was never "rolled over back to back".

The way the national currency of China is managed (on a non-free-floating basis) is another reason to steer away from using RMB as your currency of negotiation. Export factories have always been willing to negotiate and be paid in USD, and this eliminates one of the risks of operating in China.

So, a Hong Kong base allows you to focus on what's important: running and making your business successful. I'll walk you through what I've done and the logic attached to it. I went into China aggressively and later partially retracted back to Hong Kong. Regardless, Hong Kong still plays a significant role when it comes to China, even while this is slowly shifting in favour of key China cities when it comes to proximity, domestic flight costs, etc. The trick is to find a balance that works for your business. Some things are better done in Hong Kong and others in China. Right now, I have my consulting business split between Hong Kong and Shanghai, because of its adjacency to factories, and the hunger of my Mainland staff who want to be in the factories every week to chase production and negotiate the best costs. Their merchandising counterparts in Hong Kong have become too complacent, and lost the "edge" that they used to have 20 years ago. They typically prefer to sit at their desks, summoning vendors in to discuss issues—not the best way to ensure priority or guarantee on-time production.

Hong Kong Advantages:

- Amazing efficiency: In one day, you can register your business with the Companies Registry (The Hong Kong government site has straightforward instructions) and be up and running.
- Transparent legal system.
- Accounting standards integrity.
- There is a deep-seated affection from Hong Kongers for the British colonial days—indeed it is surprising how so many Hong Kongers consider the pre-handover days as being better than the current "one country—two systems". The pre-1997 workforce also participated in the widespread use of English as a second language.
- Mandarin (also called Putonghua in Chinese) is also widely spoken, and is the dominant language of business in China.
- Transparent tax system with low rates. Profits tax is capped at 16.5% and salary tax at 17%, with very little fluctuation over the years. There is no tax on dividends or capital gains.
- Transparent, efficient banking system.
- Fast and efficient broadband, and Wi-Fi and mobile phone systems without censorship, which is very different from Mainland China, where many sites such as WhatsApp, Google, Dropbox, Amazon, Facebook, Instagram, and Twitter are blocked.[1]
- Great networking opportunities.
- Conveniently located for regional travel, with multiple flights to multiple Chinese cities daily.
- Straightforward hiring of skilled staff and low cost of termination.

(continued)

- Ease of shipping product samples and goods in and out of the city with virtually no restrictions, tax, or customs clearance delays.
- Physically sharing a border with Mainland China that is a short 40-minute train ride from Central Hong Kong.
- Many senior managers who earned their degrees overseas and are very adept at managing the divide between the languages and protocols of East and West.
- Something for every lifestyle, aside from business, from a pulsing city scene to beaches and nature trails in country parks.

Hong Kong Challenges:

- Operating costs. Rent, specifically, is significantly higher for offices, typically two times the rent in China. (Comparing rent between Hong Kong and Mainland China needs careful analysis: Hong Kong uses HKD/foot/month, and China uses RMB/metre/day. Note that in both cities, landlords allocate your share of the lift lobby and aircon platforms outside the building in the space they claim they are renting to you!
- Full employment. Fortunately, there's a general unwillingness for Hong Kongers to relocate to China, which gives an advantage when it comes to hiring qualified staff in Hong Kong. You can find well-educated, professional young people. However, people in Hong Kong do have a superiority complex and think there's a

(continued)

> 10-to-1 ratio when it comes to the quality and efficiency of staff in Hong Kong versus China, so you may have to deal with some level of attitude. The costs of employment are not so different between Hong Kong and China due to the extremely expensive social welfare costs that the Chinese government requires on top of every salary. Base salary in Shanghai isn't high, but on top of that the Chinese government adds on a very high (up to 40% of base salary) loading to these initial wages for a variety of social welfare programs—maternity, accident insurance, pension, etc. The total cost of employment is therefore much higher than the take-home salary that the employee enjoys and bases their career decisions on. Indeed, my Shanghai staff have zero confidence that they will ever see any of the "benefits" that they are supposed to derive from these government welfare payments, so they don't value the benefits at all. More details are provided in Secret 6.
>
> 👎 Location. I have just pointed out the convenience of Hong Kong's proximity to China, which is reached after a mere 40-minute train ride. However, that distance still doesn't quite negate the fact that Hong Kong isn't adjacent to factories. Your Hong Kong employees won't be happy if you expect them to be at the factories across the border every day, in part because of the commute and border hassle, and in part because they're predisposed to working in an office. The mentality is very different in China where employees accept and expect to be in the factories every day. If you need people on the ground in China, then don't hire them in Hong Kong!

(continued)

- Border crossing. You can confront tens of thousands of people crossing the border on a Monday morning or Friday afternoon. This can be offset somewhat with an APEC (Asia Pacific Economic Cooperation) business travel card, but this takes time to acquire. An APEC card is essentially a business person's fast-track priority card, which allows you to enter China (and the other participating countries) without a visa and gives you access to a priority line (shared with diplomats) at immigration. (In secondary Chinese cities, I've found that the immigration staff don't necessarily understand that you don't need a visa when you have an APEC card. So even though I don't need one, I still get a three-year China visa.)
- Logistics. There is a trend for industries to move from Southern China to the North to take advantage of the roughly 20% savings in labour costs. From Hong Kong, this means a longer and more expensive flight. A ticket from Hong Kong to Beijing, for example, can often cost double compared to a domestic flight between Shenzhen, which is just across the border, and Beijing. If your future lies in Northern China, then building your operations team in Hong Kong isn't the way to go.
- English. The level of English literacy has declined in Hong Kong since the 1997 Handover when the government changed the focus in schools to Mandarin rather than English as a second language. Young people in Hong Kong today can't speak or write English as fluently in a working environment. Whereas in Shanghai, English levels are impressive and improving at great speeds.

Setting Up: A To-Do List

My first piece of advice is, don't splash out for a big physical office space in the beginning because you can't guarantee that you will have steady work as you're building your network. If you're working as a consultant, consider working from home. All my meetings are at my clients' premises. If you're still in the corporate world, you can start building your foundation with a network that includes friends and mentors. Begin to trade information with this network of experts, starting with personal recommendations to help set up shop. In the beginning, the reality is that you will be very much on your own. Your office "starter kit" should include:

- Good local lawyer and accountant (helpful for office and bank set-up).
- Secretarial service (optional).
- Financial controller.
- Travel agent for flight bookings. They work on 11% commission from the airlines and can often find you better deals. Going online using Google Flights is a good starting point, but a travel agent scores when you either have to change flights because trips need amending, or have complex multi-carrier journeys.
- Draft employment contracts.
- Draft non-disclosure agreement.

Banking Challenges in Opening an Account

A more recent development is difficulty in setting up a bank account for a new company. Even with 20 years' track record with HSBC, and a decent relationship manager for my personal banking, in late 2016 I was told that 99% of all new company account requests were rejected by HSBC. It appeared that with the added cost of compliance (anti-laundering requirements), it just wasn't profitable for some banks to take on SME-sized companies such as mine, despite a track record of zero debt, plenty of capital, and an asset-light business model.

I persevered, because I was unhappy that such an entrepreneurial place as Hong Kong wasn't supportive of new business, which I believe is the lifeblood of the economy, and eventually succeeded in opening a new company account. But I had to provide a mass of documents, including a request for a copy of the 2006 IPO I'd undertaken on the Hong Kong Stock Exchange! Not everybody wanting to start a company has the luxury of this type of documented background. However, Bank of China (HK) Ltd. has identified this indifference on the part of other large banks as a business opportunity, and is currently courting new businesses, so that may be a better first stop for you in your search for a sympathetic banker.

Staffing Up: Recruitment and Retention

It's humbling to go out on your own after being at a big corporation. When you first break out as an entrepreneur, you can't justify hiring a secretary if it's just you and you're traveling all the time. Without an executive assistant to do the essential day-to-day things for you, you'll need to add basic tasks to your to-do list.

When I first started out, for the first time in my professional life, I was booking my own airline tickets when traveling for business, shopping myself for a mobile plan for my smartphone, and working out my own budget. Thankfully, I could take a corner at a friend's office in the early days and his IT guy and accountant helped to look after me (thanks Mick!). It's a cliché, but remember that what goes around comes around, so help people out when you can.

In the beginning, you might be a one-person show, but work toward hiring staff so you'll have more free time to put toward securing new business. Once you get to that stage, remember that your new hires are taking a leap of faith with you. Instead of working for a large multinational or another established business, they are choosing to work at a start-up. This becomes a bond because the common goal is to build your business; and if you succeed, then they also succeed.

Don't make the mistake of putting someone in at the top to set the direction of your business, though. This is your job. It's essential to be involved because things change quickly and you'll miss opportunities if you aren't paying attention. The person who's passionate about the business should be driving it.

The following are factors I consider when hiring.

Team Building

It's common to change companies and take your trusted senior team with you in Asia, so build your team to last. To handle the overall organisation of your business, you'll need one personal assistant and one financial controller.

You'll also need good deputies to be your right-hand person in Hong Kong and in China. You should be able to delegate critical daily tasks to these people, who don't need to be executive level with huge salaries. Hire generalists who take initiative and are willing to turn their hand to any new opportunity that comes along that you consider worthwhile, because your office should be operating on the leanest budget possible.

Upon arriving in Hong Kong, I inherited a personal assistant named Mary. I was pleasantly shocked to discover she had a higher level of education than I did, with a law degree from Taipei University. She had previously worked as a sweater merchandiser and spoke fluent Mandarin and English, as well as her native Cantonese. I took her with me across four companies and watched her grow. She is currently running my Shanghai office as the general manager. Without her guidance and gatekeeping, I would have been completely lost and unable to relentlessly travel the way my business required in the early years.

Team building is a familiar concept in the West—less so in Asia. But it can be highly effective. During my first week of taking up my new post as general manager of merchandising at Marks & Spencer Asia, I invited my team of some 25 staff to attend an away day at a nearby hotel. Everyone was to dress casually, and the aim was to get to know each other. And also, to identify past problems and future solutions to any bottlenecks in the way the clothing and food merchandising operation for Asia was run. There were 23 women and only 2 men, which isn't unusual in our industry, and it took me a lot of effort to warm everyone up.

I started by asking everyone to share a little of their background, how they came to work for Marks & Spencer, their previous jobs, where they lived and something about their families. The Western-educated staff were more comfortable doing this, but it took some persuasion to get everyone to share about their home life. Eventually we moved on to the next phase—I asked everyone to name one thing they would change to improve their happiness at work. All proceeded normally—the first girl was unhappy about the way people returned her documents and didn't file them properly, the second disliked the computer system, etc. But the third girl simply said, "I'm 32 years old already, can you help me find a boyfriend?" I was taken aback, but managed to ask what her criteria were so I could ask my acquaintances, and she replied, "Wealthy and tall." I asked if they needed to be in a certain age range, be Western or Asian, have a sense of humour or be intelligent. She replied, "No, none of that matters. Just wealthy and tall." I thanked her for her honesty and promised to do my best! This opened the meeting to a much broader range of topics and we got to know each other better and begin bonding as a team. (I never did find her a suitable match—custom in China has it that once an unmarried woman is 27 years old she may end up a spinster).

Integrity

I'd like to address the issue of trustworthiness of staff at this point. Many Western firms want a Caucasian in charge of their Asian operation because they feel they are inherently more trustworthy than any Asian, who may cheat them out of their profits.

In my experience, people are good and bad, honest and dishonest. I've met as many Westerners who are as corrupt as Asians. It's true there are cultural differences at work, and what one Chinese person perceives as an acceptable "cash gift" or "lai see" (red packet filled with banknotes for good luck) at Chinese New Year may be shocking to a Westerner. I've seen HKD10,000 (about USD1,400) handed over to a general manager as a normal gift. Right from the start, I made it clear that whilst I wasn't prepared to ban this culturally important tradition, I was limiting it to HKD200 per donor, and anything over this amount had to be handed in to me. I'd return it and remind the supplier of our written company policy about the maximum amount permitted. Transparency lets everyone know your expectations. But bear in mind that if your staff see you being casual about pocketing gifts, or learn that you are asking your suppliers to understate their invoices to reduce duty or taxes, or overstate their invoices so you can pocket a commission, then they will consider helping themselves to some of your profits too! Act with integrity and sustain this reputation; it won't guarantee an honest staff, but it goes a long way towards defining your organisation's culture.

I've been offered a car, free holidays, a villa in Phuket, and various other inducements in my many years as a buyer—all of which were politely declined. Instead, I would ask for a further discount in the cost prices to reflect the "savings" from not having to pay such bribes. More importantly, when a proportion of my staff come forward with similar (if less lavish) tales, they are rewarded with not just the company's gratitude, but a cash bonus to incentivise others.

I'd like to share the worst area of our industry for corruption, and how I've dealt with it. Inevitably, the lowest paid jobs are the most exposed to this risk. A quality control inspector earns about USD700 per month. So, his earnings are significantly topped up with two components:

- Expenses from his travels to and from factories and overnight stays. Unfortunately, in China it is easy to buy blank receipt books that you can then fill in with any amount you want. Validating these expenses isn't easy, but with a trusted financial controller who knows what to look for (for example sequential receipt numbers from different outlets), it is possible to suppress.
- Unfortunately, it is custom for export factories to "pay to pass" final inspection so their goods can ship (and their payment be triggered). They pay a fixed fee per container to the quality control inspector. As you can imagine, this is typically a large amount compared to the inspector's monthly income, so it naturally blinds them to any potential faults that could have been caught before sending the goods overseas, and undermines the entire system.

The cure for such problems isn't outsourcing to third-party quality control companies—if anything, they are more prone to corruption, because they suffer from misalignment. You want to coach the factory to make perfect goods and ship on time, but these third-party vendors earn a fee for each inspection, so they are incentivised to reject shipments and earn an additional fee for the re-inspection.

The best solution is having a solid and loyal team of well-trained inspectors, and rotate them around your factories so no long-term relationships can be formed. In addition, you need to track the passes and failures of each inspector and factory to ensure no biases are emerging. Carefully benchmark customer complaints and returns against each inspector so that key performance indicators are tracked and published, making everyone accountable for any failures.

The Hong Kong Independent Commission Against Corruption estimates that on average, 2% of every purchase in our industry is "stolen" through corruption. I've had to deal with blatantly excessive prices being agreed on, clearly unsuitable vendors being given orders they don't deserve, and offices with falsified asset registers. So it's best to assume there is a degree of corruption in every organisation, and institute systems to limit it.

Chop Credibility

Understand that authority is vested in a company chop, or official rubber seal, which acts as a legal signature on all documents. Holding the chop gives access to all company funds, information, as well as the ability to sign contracts. Setting up signing authorities under the watchful eye of a trusted head of office is the starting point for establishing a viable business. In a foreign country where many invoices and bills are in Chinese, and the authority to pay out money from the company account is based on a single chop, the integrity of your business will be based on who has control of it, and how they use it.

Language Skills

Hire someone you can trust who can speak, read, and write Cantonese, Mandarin, and English. Personal recommendations are *far* better than interviewing unknown candidates from an agency. Regardless, it isn't easy finding someone with these language skills who is also trustworthy, but it's an essential building block to successfully working in China. The alternative is stumbling around clueless, not even able to check invoices and expenses if they're written in Chinese. However, do not make the mistake most new foreigners (including myself) have made, of mistaking a friendly demeanour and fluency in English with integrity or even competency. *Language skills are completely divorced from commercial ability.*

Cash Is King

Cash flow can consume you as an entrepreneur. This is in stark comparison to a corporate job where your budget consists of someone else's money and a pay cheque conveniently drops into your bank account every month regardless of how business is doing. Easy.

In addition to the stress of cash flow, you have no capital, no investments, no goods, and no lines of credit as a start-up business. You keep what you earn, but only when you earn! When it comes to staff, you're responsible for their salaries, health insurance, technology, and office space. No matter what you earn—or don't earn—you still need to pay your staff and related expenses at the end of the month, which is an intense consideration that's sometimes easy to underestimate when you're first starting out.

It's great when cash flows, but you need creative solutions when it goes negative. China has proved to be a great partner for these types of conversations. If you hit trouble, you must get in there with your China partner/vendor and explain things without hesitation. If you have fostered a long-term relationship with your suppliers, and they see that you are heavily involved and committed to your business while actively working on growing and keeping it healthy, then they might choose to support you by making terms more flexible.

The responsibility of having staff in Hong Kong and Shanghai in the early days made me feel like a hostage. The added costs of salaries, benefits, office space, and technology meant that to survive, I had to take work as it was offered to me. It gets worse before it gets better, but you must stick with it, rely on your staff, and focus on diversifying your portfolio. The freedom to live and work as you please will come, and with that, the pressure will begin to ease.

Feng Shui: Is It Real?

Like most foreigners I had submitted to an annual "check-up" from a feng shui master whilst working for Marks & Spencer Asia, because my Chinese staff appreciated my respect for their traditions. It felt like a blend of spiritualism, ergonomics, and hokum. When I started working for Warnaco, at my first meeting with my largest supplier, the sales director announced she was very disturbed by the vibes in my office, and insisted her feng shui master come over and visit within the next hour to correct the bad aura she detected. I was a little bemused, but agreed to meet with him as she seemed genuinely perturbed. Shortly thereafter, a wizened little old man appeared, who couldn't speak a word of English, and through my personal assistant explained that he took care of all the major clothing companies in Hong Kong, and was also paid to go to New York by some of them. His advice had seen significant improvement in business for Tommy Hilfiger, Ralph Lauren, and others, so would I let him review the office and offer his advice?

It turned out that he charged by the size of office, and Warnaco had a huge three-storey one housing over 500 staff, but the looks on my staff's face made me decide to give it a try. First, he asked to see the personnel files of all the managers so he could review their photos and birth signs. Then he announced that the (very expensive) glass door of my office needed to be relocated, and the carpet changed from blue to grey. After an hour of reviewing the staff folders, he handed me the photo of the CFO, and through my personal assistant explained that he was a thief, and that his office should be immediately relocated next to mine so I could keep a closer eye on him. The CFO was mortified, but dutifully packed up his belongings and moved down to an office next to mine, causing a domino effect as various people had to switch offices.

Two months later, an internal audit by the US finance team revealed that the CFO had been paying fake invoices from a computer supplies company owned by his wife, and the asset registry showed over 50 missing laptops. The next morning, 50 new laptops suddenly appeared in the warehouse—though they weren't of the correct manufacturer or model—and the CFO was fired. I was commended for being suspicious and making him move to the office next to mine, and alerting the audit team to my concerns. This was all triggered by the feng shui master disliking the shape of his eyebrows. It may seem unlikely, but it happened, and ever since then I've respected the advice of the *sifu* (master) and followed it. How much was intuition, how much my personal assistant's influence (who translated everything but not necessarily 100% accurately) I'll never know, but I learnt that some things defy Western logic.

IT'S ALL ABOUT PEOPLE

Setting up an office isn't difficult in Hong Kong, and it is more challenging in Mainland China. Hiring and then retaining your staff is never easy in either location—and in all likelihood, will define your success. Loyalty and integrity aren't easy to assess during an interview—only time will tell if your team possess these qualities—so focus on personal recommendations and treat head-hunters and the references they provide with commercial cynicism. I always interview ever member of staff we hire, irrespective of seniority, and for managers, always personally ring their past employer to discuss why they want to move and what their real strengths and weaknesses are. Phone discussions reveal far more than written reference responses.

SUMMARY

- Understand the different roles of a Hong Kong office and a Mainland China office, and how they complement each other.
- Keep it lean—adapt the "to-do" setup checklist and stick to it. Avoid vanity spending on luxurious offices or support staff.
- Only three things matter—people, people, and people. Their recruitment and retention is the lifeblood of your business.

SECRET FIVE: PARTNERING FOR PROFIT

>  Same bed, different dreams.
>
> Chinese proverb

This chapter begins with Wes going into partnership with his largest customer. The attractions of teaming up with other businessmen can be compelling—accelerating your growth and complementing your strengths with theirs—but a shared dream can turn into a nightmare. Lessons to be Learnt then moves on to consider the criteria best used to assess potential partners, and some of the mistakes I have made that need to be avoided.

WES PARTNERS UP

Staring down at the hefty prenuptial agreement in his hands, Wes reflected on his previous two failed marriages, and wondered if this time would be any different. "Once the honeymoon wears off", he mused, "and the realities of normal life begin, you never know what will happen, and this stack of paper won't help much." Wes was a realist, and his previous divorces had been costly in dollars as well as self-esteem and emotional well-being. His best friend and lawyer sat across the table, and he had insisted on a full contract that attempted to foresee every potential pitfall and pre-negotiate any future separation settlement—but that hardly seemed the spirit in which to embark on a new relationship. Still, Paul kept reminding him that 50% of all marriages ended in divorce, and the rate for second and third marriages was even worse, so what choice did he have?

Suddenly Paul coughed, reminding Wes that if he hadn't been such an old friend he would be charging by the hour, and daydreaming for 10 minutes whilst gazing out of the legal firm's 42nd floor office at the harbour view below was an expensive luxury. Wes refocused and looked across the conference table; in front of him were three documents—a 150-page shareholder agreement (that Wes referred to as a prenuptial agreement), a 10-page employment contract installing him as the CEO of the new joint venture, and a two-page loan agreement that his potential partners were injecting USD5 million into the new business as working capital.

Wes regretted that it had taken over nine months to get to this stage. His largest customer, with a chain of 200 stores in the US, had proposed that they merge their Asian sourcing operations because each had staff and offices in Hong Kong and Shanghai. That alone wouldn't have tempted Wes, but he had a secret ambition to serve other (non-competing) customers with their offices, thereby converting his Asian base from a cost to a profit centre in one fell swoop.

Wes dreamt of freeing up his balance sheet, leveraging his investment in Asia, and eventually getting his sourcing operation for free! His partners were equally enthusiastic, but were insistent that he had to run the whole Asian operation, and find the third-party customers. "Fair enough," thought Wes, "this could be the start of something big."

Wes's impending partner was double his size, and they were guaranteeing that all their sourcing would go through the new setup on a 10% commission basis. They were providing the working capital for the new joint venture, so both parties had agreed they would own two-thirds of the new company. There were to be three directors: Wes, Chairman Dick, and his younger brother Mark. They'd reassured Wes that the company would be run by him day-to-day. It had to meet board-set targets, but any significant decision required a "super-majority", meaning Wes could block anything he didn't like. Over half the document referred to what would happen if and when one of the parties decided to exit—the remaining one had right of first refusal to buy—and they had negotiated hard to establish in advance the exact valuation: 6.5 times earnings before interest, taxes, depreciation, and amortisation (EBITDA), so the formula was set and everyone knew where they stood.

One concern causing Wes to mistrust Dick was why they needed a 150-page shareholder agreement for this modestly-sized sourcing and buying agency operation. They weren't a global conglomerate. If Wes had needed to pay Paul his going rate for sorting out the agreement, he would never have embarked on this scheme. Even his staff weren't happy to be merged into another larger company's operations; he'd only persuaded them to come along because of loyalty, and the fact that he'd be overall boss. Julie, his general manager, was scathing about working in a larger company; she had joined Wes to escape the politics and bureaucracy of corporate life, and here was Wes embracing it again.

Still, Wes mused, he'd always fancied himself a medium-size fish in a big bowl rather than a big fish in a little bowl, and now he had a platform to accelerate his business and alleviate the irritatingly large overhead of staff and rent he was carrying in Hong Kong and Shanghai. What could go wrong? Pretty much every eventuality had been written into the agreement, including if he sold his own business or his partners did.

Still, as Paul coughed again and handed him a pen, the analogy to a pre-nuptial agreement caused Wes to pause. He'd had one for his second marriage, and that hadn't helped. Would this be different? Wes shrugged off his doubts and signed.

* * *

Fast-forward four years, and Wes was back in Paul's office combing through the Shareholder Agreement and seeking advice on how to negotiate his exit. It was proving anything but straightforward. Wes was reminded of the joke about the American tourists lost in the Irish countryside. Eventually they find a farmer and ask him, "How do we get back to our hotel?"

"Well," says the farmer. "I wouldn't start here."

Dick had turned out to be an arrogant bully, humiliating his family members and staff alike. Mark was his mouthpiece and towed the line. And relations were strained to say the least. The ability to block key decisions hadn't helped anyone, and Dick's endless insistence that Wes recruit a top-notch CEO for "succession planning purposes" was a poorly cloaked attempt to prepare for Wes's departure. Wes had requested he be bought out at the pre-agreed 6.5 multiple of last year's EBITDA and submitted his figures to the board. Dick countered by saying that "profits needed to be normalised" and submitted an outrageous set of accounts that almost zero-ised the profit for the last few years, claiming that the joint venture had been overcharging his company for the entire time and that it had to be reversed before calculating the EBITDA. Wes had hired a Big Four accounting company in Hong Kong to confirm that Dick's normalisation was completely irrational, but each party refused to back down, and now Wes was hoping Paul had a bright idea on how to break the deadlock.

LESSONS TO BE LEARNT

Choosing the Right Partner

Founding a successful partnership requires both attraction and retention. A decade ago, attraction was the more difficult side of the equation. Retention was easy. Now, it's reversed. Want to find a Chinese supplier? Search Alibaba.com and you'll find a list of them, but be careful wading through the sea of brokers, sales agencies, and others posing as factories. Good old-fashioned networking is usually how you'll find the best partners. A lot of it is following your gut feeling, but if you pay attention to what you see and what is said, you can put together an accurate sense of someone and their business.

Let's work through the list of what Wes did and didn't find in his future partner.

Complimentary Skills, Channels to Market, Networks

Obviously, it makes sense to "marry" a partner that can bring to the table what you lack, and vice versa. This might mean manufacturing expertise from your China partner and product development, complemented by sales and marketing channels, from yourself. But as we saw in Wes's case, it was really the additional volume for sourcing and the synergistic savings predicted that indicated a potentially good fit.

Naturally, you will want to ensure there is no channel conflict with your potential partner by asking whether they have a lot of sales in the region you supply. Are they already dealing with your competition? Do they have a strong relationship with your competition?

Financial Wherewithal

Often, knowing which city your potential partner comes from and their family's standing will give you a good indication of how well-off he or she is—because China is all about connections. Through your getting-to-know-you conversations, find out: which city they're from; what businesses their families are involved in; their industry background; and their family's standing. Use your network. Ensure you get a personal reference. Wes got this right—his partner was willing to invest USD5 million, injecting working capital in the form of a loan into the joint venture, saving Wes from using up his own cash.

Shared Expectations

With the benefit of hindsight, Wes's joint venture with Dick was doomed from the start. Far too much emphasis was made on downside protection, when no amount of contract protection can overcome a misalignment of goals. Dick was pompous and wanted to be "a global business leader". Wes simply wanted to expand his reach and offset the costs of the sourcing operation. Both parties signing up for a business plan projection for the next five years, listing key performance indicators and goals for sales, costs, and profit, would have helped manage expectations and ensured a shared ambition and interest to grow.

It is usually easy to find ambition. The trick is to ensure that you and your business partners have the *same* ambition! Alignment is key if a long-term relationship is going to work. Does he or she simply want access to customers, in which case you've outlived your usefulness once those introductions are made, or do they require your help with product development and marketing? Do they understand and appreciate the value that you bring to their organisation? How can you sustain the relationship once the "honeymoon period" is over?

Energy

Doing business in today's climate isn't easy. A positive, energetic owner will make the best partner for the challenges and opportunities ahead. You shouldn't be expected to do all the work. Wes found himself stuck in a relationship where he was expected to make all of the running, and Dick sat back and criticised. This isn't likely to lead to long-term success.

A Good Attitude

If your potential partner doesn't have this, then everything will crash and burn. I can't stress enough how important this requirement is for a great long-term China partner. Things will go wrong, and that's why you and your partner are needed—to resolve problems.

Common Values

Does your potential partner have similar values? Do they have integrity? Do they treat their staff well? Do they delegate making appointments to their secretary or make arrangements themselves? Does he or she delegate a lot in general? (This might be an indication for how well you'll be taken care of. You want the owner's attention.) Do they respond to e-mails/communications in a timely manner? Is there a management team to work with if the big boss is away? If not, is the boss available by phone?

Are they trustworthy? Organised and disciplined? Punctual? If they make their meetings on time, their production is more likely to be on time. Anyone who works for themselves values time, so it's a matter of respect.

In choosing the right partner in Asia, it is important to identify which *type* of partner you prefer—it is simplistic but valid to say that the typical Hong Kong business person understands the West better, and operates under familiar colonial law, but is more risk-averse. His or her counterpart in Mainland China is comfortable operating in a less formatted environment, and tolerates a higher risk-to-reward ratio.

I recently asked my advisory board, consisting of five Hong Kong and Mainland Chinese businessmen, what they thought was the key difference between Hong Kong and Mainland business owners. There was unanimous agreement—Hong Kongers first look at the *downside* risk of a potential investment. Mainlanders look at the potential *upside*, and will figure out how to make it work as it goes along. Increased market share and first-mover advantage are worth significant risk to them.

I have also witnessed an increasing number of Hong Kong businessmen in recent years selling their factories to Mainlanders. The simple reason—Mainlanders drive their workforces much harder, and in a much more Mao/Stalinesque style, which is not the way Hong Kongers (with their East meets West education and moral codes) typically operate. Hence, these factories, once sold, can operate in a far more productive and cost-effective way.

In this chapter's example, Wes chose to partner with an American company, so he was dealing with his native citizens. But you might be considering a partnership with a Chinese company to better complement the Western networks and techniques that you bring to the table. So, understanding the difference between Hong Kong and Mainland thought processes will be critical to managing your risk and expectations.

Choosing the Right Partnership Model

Many factories offer shares to their major customers in the hope that it will "bind" their customers to them. I never accept these proposals as I have no interest in being a minority shareholder in a private Mainland Chinese company with opaque shareholders, governance, and accounting.

A joint venture, however, with a newly created entity that both partners own 50:50 of and is registered in Hong Kong is a very different beast, and ring-fenced from the other Mainland business that your potential partner owns. As long as it is subject to the laws and accounting rules of Hong Kong, your level of protection is dramatically improved. Chinese operations can be subsidiaries of the Hong Kong entity that are either representative offices or wholly owned foreign enterprises, depending on the projected size of turnover, investment, and headcount.

In terms of the type of business model to have when considering a partnership, these are the criteria that I look out for:

- "Asset light"—doesn't require significant stock-holding or purchase of goods in advance so cash flow is positive. You typically get paid before you have to pay your factories.
- Fixed costs are small; variable costs dominate. You only spend more once you have firm orders.
- Not a "single leg" stool. Always have at least three customers and be working on your pipeline to be able to replace at least one.
- Niche player rather than a generalist; it makes you more unique.
- Significant barrier to entry.
- "Push on an open door." Obviously don't back contracting trends; choose growth opportunities. (I seek out Internet retailers rather than department stores.)
- Blend monthly income with an element of ownership so you can participate in the upside. A steady income stream is important, but so is receiving a reward when a brand you've helped build takes off.

Avoiding Being Cheated

Whenever you talk about doing business in China, inevitably someone has a story about how they got screwed. Yes, there are many stories of unscrupulous Chinese factories deceiving Western partners. Take your pick: fake factories set up or borrowed to present a palatable image, factory workload manipulated to make the lines seem full, raw materials substituted without your knowledge to save money and improve the factory's margins, etc.

But at the core of it, it's simply a relationship that needs to be managed properly. Don't buy into the popular belief that you'll be cheated at every turn. Your Chinese partners want to be successful and they want you to be successful as their partner. It's a mutually beneficial relationship if you handle it with the right attitude and a reasonable approach.

It's important to know the competitive landscape, set realistic and achievable goals in terms of prices and delivery, and then push the factory hard to meet your expectations. If you demand excessively low prices, an unrealistically quick delivery, or ridiculously high-quality standards, then yes, you'll be screwed. The factory might accept the job if work is slow at that time, but then drop your order at the last minute when a more profitable order comes along.

When this happens, the fault mostly lies with you for being unrealistic, not the factory. This is where you must adapt your thinking. The factory will tell you what you want to hear, which is technically lying. But whether they lie is neither here nor there. The key is to understand that the Chinese mentality is to say, "Can," and then figure out how to do it later. It's a wonderfully positive approach, but can lead to disappointment. Reasonable requests generally translate to expectations that are successfully met.

The single biggest request I receive from potential clients is to help safeguard their China operations from the "endemically corrupt grip of Chinese staff and factories". They act as if the Chinese invented corruption and think a Western face running the show guarantees some sort of ethical behaviour. It doesn't. Having a foreigner in control gives a false sense of security to many Western companies. Where opportunity exists, human greed will follow, regardless of ethnicity. You safeguard your business with excellent staff and trusting relationships with your partners.

My Many Failures and What They Taught Me

It is worthwhile to focus on my failures—and the need to "fail fast" when ideas don't gel and business plans can't be met. I've invested in a wide variety of businesses; some stalled on take-off, others burnt a lot of fuel before gently falling back to earth, and one or two exploded on impact, but the lessons I learnt weren't wasted:

- I helped found a cloud-based media storage company. The CEO was a technical genius, but he failed to develop the application in a way that generated income. 250,000 people were using the service when we pulled the plug, but barely anybody paid. We had a high-profile investor, but no prospects of a healthy revenue to cover costs, and the US Silicon Valley model of achieving high valuations for customer numbers rather than cash flow eluded us.
- Family-owned companies run by Chinese patriarchs who hold an IPO and then refuse to acknowledge the role of shareholders is a common problem, and I have served on several boards where I struggled to persuade the majority owner as to the rights of the minority shareholders.
- Setting up and optimising buying offices in Shanghai, my consulting company's expertise, hasn't always resulted in a leaner and faster organisation or process. "Rubbish in, rubbish out" is a familiar term in computing but it applies just as much to procurement. Ask for an

inferior product, or a ludicrously low price, and don't be surprised when you are disappointed. The best operations work in partnership between head office and Asian offices, but all too frequently they work in opposition of each other, playing "the blame game" when results disappoint.

Still, I believe that niche consulting, where we lend our expertise not just to the discovering of what needs changing, but also implementing those changes on behalf of clients, is the future. Delivering recommendations but failing to stick around for the far harder part, implementing them, seems inappropriate and old-fashioned. Most companies already know what is wrong and roughly how to change it. Our role is partly cheerleader, partly bench-marker, and partly energiser of change.

CONCLUSION

The partnership route can definitely accelerate your growth plans, and if the two partners and their businesses are complementary, then it can be a case of 2+2=5. But select your partner with care, using the criteria in this chapter, and learn from my many failures so that you improve the odds of a successful venture.

Manage your expectations, and if you feel you are being taken advantage of, explore why it is happening and try and work out a resolution that addresses both parties' issues. Try to remember that in any disagreement, it is *never* all one party's fault.

Finally, be sure to run your new business under Hong Kong and not Mainland Chinese rule of law and accounting standards.

SUMMARY

- Now may be the right time to find long-term partners in China to accelerate your growth. Be meticulous and use the checklist under Choosing the Right Partner to assess potential partners.
- Ensure your business model is appropriate. 50:50 joint ventures are clean, simple, and easily understood.
- Choose a business model suited to today's environment. Making goods in the hope of selling them is antiquated.
- Contracts are of limited use as fall-backs. Expecting reasonable behaviour during a divorce based on set of rules negotiated during a honeymoon is unrealistic.
- For new business ideas, fail *fast* if they don't meet your target.

SECRET SIX:
COPING WITH CHALLENGES

> *When it is obvious that your goals cannot be reached, don't adjust your goals; adjust your actions.*
>
> Confucius

This chapter addresses the major concerns that Western companies have before entering China. We start with Wes grappling with the complexities of the law. Then in Lessons to Be Learnt, we cover the challenges presented by the legal system (including intellectual property rights), social compliance, and common supplier problems. Finally, we consider how to choose the right structure for your business, how to get your money out, and how to deal with currency fluctuations.

WES HITS A ROADBLOACK

"He said *what*?" Wes screamed at Julie. There was silence from Julie; she didn't know what to say. She was standing in Canton Fair in Guangzhou, the largest trade show in the world, where every six months 20,000 vendors show their wares to 100,000 buyers from all over the world.

Julie had been sent to find some new, more competitive sources for their novelty products that were popular with Wes's US big box customers, and increasingly popular on Amazon. The first stall she had approached, Tunnel Plastics, had been most welcoming—because they claimed they were already supplying Wes! It seems they were the actual factory making their products, and Julie had been dealing with middleman Post Productions, whom she and Wes thought were the factory. This infuriated Wes because he expected Julie to go straight to the manufacturer, not use trading companies that were then outsourcing their production and marking up the factory price with their own commission. And to make matters worse, Tunnel were showing potential customers Wes's new designs. He had agreed to pay Post Productions USD20,000 for the moulds to be developed. And here it was, freely on show at Canton Fair before his customers had sold a single item.

Julie was still on the line, waiting for Wes to cool down. She had been surprised that the factory was supplying them without her knowing it, but unlike Wes, she wasn't shocked they were offering their designs to others. After all, the main reason Wes had sent Julie to the Fair was to spy on their competitors, get their brochures, and order some samples. He had even had some fake business cards printed so she wouldn't have to reveal whom she really worked for. Wes didn't see the irony in complaining about others doing what he was encouraging her to do.

Julie knew Wes would demand legal action, and that the only winner would be the lawyers. She had been down this road before. Lawyers always claimed they could make a case and cause the offender to cease and desist, but wouldn't work on a success-only fee, and got paid more the longer the legalities dragged on.

LESSONS TO BE LEARNT

Having looked in earlier chapters at the many positive and rewarding aspects to working in China, here we address the significant challenges that need to be mitigated. It isn't a straight shot to success when you choose to work in a highly competitive environment with wild business cycles and a different culture and language to your own. Understand what you're up against so that you can plan your response.

In the anecdote above, if Wes had gained a better understanding of the Chinese legal system and intellectual property protection in China, he would have been more realistic about his options, and better protected.

Let's go through some common scenarios and review what your response might be.

China's Legal Structure

The Chinese legal system is a civil law system based on written statutes. Unlike the common law legal system used in most Western countries, *prior court decisions have little value*. Furthermore, China's statutes are subject to interpretation by legislative bodies, judicial authorities, and enforcement bodies, which increases the uncertainty of any outcome. Since 1978, when the Chinese government started economic reforms, China began developing laws and regulations in relation to foreign investment, corporate organisation and governance, import and export, commercial transactions, taxation and trade. Many of these laws and regulations are relatively new and are subject to frequent changes and uncertainties in implementation and interpretation.

What this means is that when you bring a lawsuit, the judge assigned takes the law and interprets how it applies to your case afresh each time. Both parties submit a written proposal stating how they believe the law applies, and the judge then rules. In my experience, it is *highly* unlikely that a judge will look as favourably on a Western complainant as a Chinese defendant, irrespective of the fact that you are being represented by a local Mainland law firm. That's just reality. And Chinese judges are, relative to the West, extremely lowly paid, so the potential for influencing them is higher. All this makes "going legal" a lottery if you are in Mainland China.

Hong Kong, under the handover agreement with the UK, retains a broadly unchanged legal system till 2047, maintaining transparency, judicial independence, and the common law system of prior cases setting precedence. This reinforces the importance of using Hong Kong law wherever possible. But if you can't, and you feel the need to take legal action in Mainland China, make sure your chosen law firm in Hong Kong has a branch in Shanghai and Beijing, and can arrange a conference call to determine your options.

I've had extensive experience of lawsuits in Mainland China due to chairing a Chinese venture capital fund where a number of investments went wrong, and have learnt the hard way the virtual impossibility of winning a case. In the only major arbitration case we did win, we found collecting the proceeds from a publicly listed Mainland company impossible. The only silver lining was that in every case, whilst we did have to pay our lawyers a retainer, they agreed to reduce their fees somewhat and share in the proceeds if the case were successful. (In the solitary case we won, we ended up having to pay our lawyer's bonus even though we never collected our damages!) So, the lesson learnt is, *don't bother taking legal action in Mainland China*. It won't do anything but make you feel better that you are taking action, and line your lawyer's pockets. The mantra for when things go wrong with your partner, supplier, or staff in the Mainland is, *"If you have to pull out and consult the contract to see what protection it gives you, it's too late to salvage the situation."*

Intellectual Property Rights Protection

A major cause of concern for most of my clients is whether their Chinese vendors will be selling off their unique products or concepts to competitors. A significant number will if they believe they can get away with it. How can you protect yourself? Legal protection is scant and unreliable for the reasons explained above *if* the vendor is a Mainland company. But if they (and you) are a Hong Kong entity, then there is greater clarity on the costs and outcomes possible, and it may be worth at least starting legal proceedings to demonstrate your seriousness.

I've never experienced success where a Western customer successfully brings a lawsuit against a local Chinese vendor, because the court system favours the Chinese firm. However, there are steps you can take to protect yourself.

Legal Protection as a Last Resort

Firstly, your best bet is to rely on your relationship with the factory owner. If he believes it is in his best interest to work with you, he will protect the integrity of your intellectual property. Avoiding "going legal" should be your first instinct.

Secondly, there are legal steps available that may assist. Intellectual property registration of trademarks, copyrights, and patents can all be undertaken in China, and an experienced law firm can assist with choosing an intellectual property ownership structure for a fee.

Intellectual Property Protection History

In order to help you determine the best route for your company, here's a quick summary of the intellectual property protection history in China:

Intellectual property rights (IPRs) have been acknowledged and protected in China since 1979. The People's Republic of China has acceded to the major international conventions on protection of rights to intellectual property, but despite this, copyright violations are common. The American Chamber of Commerce in China surveyed over 500 of its members doing business regarding IPR for its "2016 China Business Climate Survey Report". The results showed that its members thought that China's intellectual property protection laws were excellent, but their enforcement was weak.[1]

The legal framework for protecting intellectual property in China is built on three separate national laws passed by the National People's Congress but administered by three completely different bodies: the Patent Law (administered by the State Intellectual Property Office), the Trademark Law (administered by the State Administration for Industry and Commerce), and the Copyright Law (administered by the State Administration for Press and Publication Implementation).

To handle cases of infringement of IPRs more efficiently, special intellectual property courts have been established in some cities and provinces. At the level of the Higher People's Court in Beijing, Shanghai, Guangdong, Fujian, and Hainan, intellectual property courts have been separated from the economic division. Beijing, Shanghai, and Tianjin have also established intellectual property courts within the Intermediate People's Court.

Despite this regulation existing as a legislative capacity, the ability to enforce these laws varies according to the differing interpretations that exist amongst the local governmental authorities in China. Despite the growing number of raids on hubs for traders of counterfeited goods and the rise in the number of lawsuits brought against companies that use counterfeited technology, codes, or logos, the level of government response does not match the degree to which counterfeiting is happening in China. There is little awareness that IPR infringement is a crime.

Intellectual Property Protection Strategy

So, what can you do to protect yourself? Just sit back and play nice? That wouldn't be a reassuring strategy. I'd recommend a four-step approach to protection as advocated by George Yip and Bruce McKern:[2]

- If you have any intention of using it within China, you should patent in China any intellectual property that has been registered elsewhere. As patents are national rights, this is an essential requirement. Failure to do so can result in Chinese (or other) competitors learning about the technology from, for example, published US patents, which they can then freely exploit in the local environment.
- Adopt best practices to protect inflow and outflow of sensitive classes of material, such as by monitoring computers and laptops (and blocking their USB ports), and banning mobile phones in the workplace—a common Chinese tactic. Secrecy agreements with employees and suppliers are also recommended.
- Split R&D into modular tasks and allocate core tasks to the headquarters group, with only specific tasks allocated to the group in China. Although this requires close collaboration between R&D headquarters and the China R&D centre, it can provide protection, as the research can be compartmentalised.
- The best protection is to have highly motivated employees who want a long-term career with the company and who want to align their futures with it. Of course, it is impossible to stop an employee walking out the door to work for a competitor, but a well-thought-out retention policy can help. Remember that Chinese staff are generally loyal to their *boss*, not the company.

Please do not place any reliance on non-compete clauses in your staffs' contracts—they are virtually worthless in either Hong Kong or China, where past experience demonstrates that the courts favour the employees' need to work, rather than the threat to the employer's business.

Social Compliance

As with intellectual property protection, China has some of the world's best legislation for the protection of workers, as befits a socialist economy. However, the implementation of this protection is limited at best.

As an example, it is illegal for anyone to work more than 60 hours a week, or not to rest on the seventh day. However, it is almost impossible to find a factory that implements this all year round. The pressure that builds from December to February, when factories close for the three-week annual Chinese New Year shutdown, means every factory is working flat out to ship goods before the holidays.

So how can you protect your brand from breaking the law, or being perceived as using sweatshop labour? Be honest about your reason for wanting a code of conduct. Most large companies do it to keep their shareholders and board onside, rather than because of a deep-seated, caring approach to the workers making their brand. Or, they do it to protect the brand's image from headlines showing underage or mistreated workers making expensive Western products.

If you simply want to ensure you can sleep at night knowing no children were involved in making your goods, and that your workers were treated with respect and within the laws of the China, then decide where you can be flexible in implementing your code, and don't expect to get these restrictive labour practices for free. Compliance costs money. Those are just the facts. I'd argue that it is a price well worth paying, but you have to decide your own approach. I've experienced prison labour being used, underage children working alongside their mothers during the school holidays, toilet breaks being restricted, passports/ID cards being withheld, and even a worker dying because the factory manager refused to let her go home when ill. So I strongly believe it is important to source ethically or not at all. But it is a craft, not a science.

The first step is to adopt your own code of conduct. Most Western brands have similar codes, so start by reviewing theirs, or take a look at my own company's code on our website, www.55brandmgmt.com.

Decide what is important to you and stick to it, ensuring every management member of your staff and your suppliers signs off on it, stating that they understand and are responsible for implementing it. Then, it requires constant auditing and follow-up with corrective action plans. The most common violations are excessive overtime and lack of seventh day rest. My own approach is based on finding factories where the owner has a positive attitude, and we can coach him and his staff to achieve our goals, rather than police and fail them when they violate our code. Every factory has its problems; what you must do is work with them to eliminate those that aren't acceptable. However, we do maintain a list of "zero tolerance" behaviours, such as using workers under the age of 16, and enforced overtime.

Over the years I've seen many tricks that factories use to pass our compliance audits—coaching workers on how to answer auditors' questions, but leaving a copy of the "answers" in the photocopier, or having a clerk stamp the timecards for every worker, resulting in 2,000 workers all miraculously clocking in at 8.02am every day!

Supplier Issues

Changing the Rules in Their Favour (Without Informing You)

If you've negotiated a very mean price and the vendor agrees to it, then don't be surprised when they swap to a cheaper material, subcontract to another factory, or are lax with timing if a more lucrative order comes in. If this is your definition of being cheated, then yes, it happens. But you must consider that if you negotiate hard with them, then they're going to push back with you even more. It's a game that is played—and one you will lose—if you aren't reasonable with your demands. The most important thing to remember is that it's about building trust with your vendors. The way you respond if a factory subcontracts your order or swaps components is also tied into the notion of building trust. Understand that while it might seem like a betrayal on the factory's part, this doesn't have to be the end of your relationship.

Subcontracting

You go to a nice factory and it looks great in regards to social compliance and in comparison to other factories. You place an order. The factory boss then subcontracts the work out to multiple outside factories because his production lines are swamped. These sub-vendor factories are often a disaster when it comes to quality, safety, and social-compliance issues. You're now in a position where you can't guarantee consistency, quality, or social compliance to your customers. When it's subcontracted, you simply don't have access to that information, which is a major problem. As usual, you send your quality control people and try to make sure things are happening as they should. But if a job is indeed subcontracted, you often find out issues when it's too late.

You must constantly work at peeling back the many layers in China to understand what's going on. While you may be angry and frustrated, go to the factory boss and ask him to be honest about what the problem is, and then reassure him that you'll help to work with the other subcontracted factory this time. In the early stages, you'll be taking cues from each other. His methods as the two of you move forward will depend on how you handle problems. Likewise, if the vendor is honest with you, then you'll be more inclined to help if he runs into trouble the next time. Work toward building a trusting relationship so the vendor is less likely to hide issues or lie to you in the future. In any case, there's never a situation where it's OK to disrespect the boss in front of his people; this weakens his position of authority and will affect his eagerness to work with you long-term.

We experienced the issue of subcontracting recently at a plastic inflatables factory. After Chinese New Year, they reported that they had suffered a fire in their warehouse and had lost 30% of their capacity. I dispatched a trusted manager from our Shanghai office to Yi Wu where they were based. Her assessment was that it was a fake fire, that had been created in the corner of their warehouse as an excuse for delayed production, and the photos she took supported this interpretation. During the week afterward, she was able to investigate the status of raw material and packaging inventory and discovered that 80% of the production had been subcontracted to very small factories, who were being paid substantially less for their work, and who had therefore failed to prioritise our products. Rather than be honest about the subcontracting and loss of control, the factory owner had lied. My manager took control of the order processing and assigned subcontractors we had used before to take on the work, albeit at higher cost to the original manufacturer, and the USD6 million order was saved, but only by us having someone permanently stationed in the factory who reported daily output, so we could manage our customer's expectations. We withheld a buffer in case of customer claims and until the order was completed, and levied a penalty on the cost prices due to the factory's failure to manage our orders.

Swapping Components

Again, if you've negotiated an unreasonably cheap price, then there's a very real possibility that your vendor will switch components for a cheaper option to cut costs and increase the factory's margin. It's typical, for example, to get a sweater that is 20% cashmere when you requested

60%. But this is also typical of a new relationship. You cannot cut out every factory that does this to you because there won't be any left for you to work with. We haven't found any factories that don't try to push the boundaries of using recycled or scrap material in greater portions compared with virgin material. Treat it as a game in which you must detect likely downgrades and ensure the original specifications are upheld.

What should you do when you discover components being changed? Take a deep breath, and then sit down with the factory boss to talk about why it happened, how to prevent it, and what the cost implications will be. Again, try to build trusting relationships so they won't hide issues or lie to you. In the end, do a final inspection to make sure the components haven't been downgraded. It isn't always easy, but try to find honest quality control people to work for you.

Supply and Demand Impacting Cost Prices

Pricing is dependent on supply and demand. It's easy to find yourself in a situation where there's a major overreaction, whether up or down, particularly when it comes to raw materials. When China started investing in infrastructure to jumpstart its economy, for example, people started to buy aluminium and copper. Then US investors started investing in these raw materials' futures. Vendors don't have a lot of inventory or credit availability, so they simply can't afford to buy excess stock. This all makes them feel nervous because they can't afford to absorb any fluctuation in raw materials with such small margins. In the end, they have no choice but to adjust their prices.

For example, silk prices in the beginning of 2011 started going up dramatically—40% in a week. We didn't understand why this was happening at first, but eventually discovered that land-development projects in the Yangtze delta were clearing away mulberry bushes in areas that silk worms fed. The following week, the price went up by 80%

and I started to see bolts of silk in the office behind people's desks as my staff started hoarding! It eventually hit 120% because people overreacted and did exactly what my staff did with what was available. To combat this, we moved to production in polyester (a man-made equivalent that when "peached" can closely resemble silk) and watched as the price of silk started coming down.

A more recent example was the surge in plastic prices in the autumn of 2016. Oil was weak and hovering around USD50 a barrel, yet plastic/ton was spiking at over RMB12,000 versus RMB9,000 a year ago. Vendors were calling for major cost price increase to cover their losses, but it didn't make sense. One maxim when analysing prices is not to trust your manufacturers because it is in their interests to present escalating costs. My clients did not panic or accept these increases, because they defied logic, and we were hopeful that the price would ease after the peak production just before Chinese New Year in February 2017. Fortunately, this forecast came true, and my clients could suppress the clamour for increases.

Increasing Labour Costs

Headlines are filled with articles about China's rising labour cost. And it's true: China is no longer the cheap factory to the world. Annually, the cost of labour increases between 14% and 21%, which undermines China's viability.

But its impact depends upon the specific product, because everything requires different amounts of labour. I discovered as director of a Hong Kong electronics manufacturer that for TV remote controls, for example, the labour cost is just 2% of the total price. On the other hand, the labour cost of complicated dresses can be up to 50%. The company that makes remote controls is happy to continue working in South China, where it's more expensive, because labour as a component is small. But if you're making dresses, you're going to die in the south. You had better head north where labour is about 10% cheaper.

The effect can be neutralised or at least partially mitigated if other Asian economies also adopt similar wage increases. I've seen many examples where other countries such as Vietnam and Cambodia embrace and implement what China puts into practice, thereby neutralising the impact of China's increase.

There is no way to get around this. It will affect your bottom line, so it becomes even more important to understand what percentage labour occupies when you're negotiating prices. Work directly with your China partners to understand their strengths and weaknesses, and identify areas of efficiency and savings. They will welcome your involvement—a win-win situation.

I just recently oversaw price negotiations with a plastic toy manufacturer that had stalled with an American customer. Neither the Western brand owner nor the factory owner would compromise. I began by making sure I understood the parameters: silicone costs and carton costs had both surged in recent months—partly due to directives from Beijing to curtail polluting industries—the former by 30+% and the latter by 50+%. But I also made sure both parties understood that the retail market in the US couldn't stand any price increase. I began by asking the owner if she would like to discuss this problem in an antagonistic way, or as partners. She immediately said she preferred the latter. I explained that the prices she had quoted were reasonable, but unfortunately unacceptable. She had simply added 10 cents onto every price from last year, so inevitably it was a large increase of around 8% for low cost products, but a more reasonable 3% for more expensive items. I explained we needed an "across the board" price agreement based on a percentage reduction from the last quoted prices, and we agreed to work though the list of some 12 items representing USD5 million of orders. As we struggled on the first item, I gave in to a higher percentage increase because it was a relatively small order, but when it came to the big items I was firmer. We ended up agreeing to an across-the-board 3.3% reduction on the quoted prices. I thanked her for her cooperation and asked what I could do in return—she produced two old invoices for modest amounts that had never been paid, and I immediately authorised payment. There was no point driving her to the point of supplication where I felt I'd won and she felt she'd lost, because I had to rely on her to make the orders for the next nine months, and hopefully for the next nine years!

The Power of Patience

There is one big difference between Western companies and Chinese operations that bring many businesses in China to their knees before they can develop: the perspective of time. Chinese executives and entrepreneurs view events with a longer time frame than Western executives, who seem to live and die by quarterly earnings reports and key performance indicators. If you think you are going to "seal the deal" with a new Chinese supplier in one quick trip, like Wes did in our Secret 1 example, then you're going to be disappointed. I learned this through my own disappointments with many failed first visits. When I was flying in from London as a merchandise manager to "seal a deal", I always wanted to demonstrate the impact my visit had made to my boss—but it rarely worked out so quickly.

While China's rapid growth might seem unlikely when you consider the painfully slow process for getting initial relationships up and running, Chinese factories can wow you with their fast turnaround time. Western companies often take weeks to turn around modified samples while new prototypes can be produced in a matter of days in China factories.

Be patient in the beginning as you get to know your vendors. It's a good investment to spend time with them, eat with them, and get to know them. Find out what they really want or need from your relationship. This is the most important thing you can do for your business.

A recent situation occurred in which the American sourcing director of one of my clients met with a factory owner he was anxious to grow with, and was disappointed that he only wanted to do USD1 million of business in the first year. But when I queried my senior manager who had accompanied him on his visit, it transpired that the sourcing director had been arrogant, and the owner had instructed his staff to cap their business at USD1 million because he felt uneasy about the intent of the American. So, the Chinese manager and I called the owner and explained our business plan and the immediate need for more capacity, and he swiftly agreed to undertake USD3-5 million in the first year, providing the American wasn't involved. This underlines the importance of dealing only with the owner of the business, and of selling what you can do for the vendor. I then had the delicate task of explaining to the boss of the American company that his sourcing director wasn't sufficiently experienced to optimise their purchasing in China, and needed oversight and training.

RMB Fluctuation

The RMB is a hybrid currency managed by Beijing but with a limited band of flexibility. The trading price of the US dollar against the RMB was allowed to float within a narrow margin of 0.3% beginning in 2005. In 2007, the margin was extended to 0.5%. In 2012, the margin was extended to 1.0%, and in 2014, the margin was extended to 2%.[3]

Not only is the exchange rate controlled in China, but the *amount* of money that can be converted is controlled. From 2010, Chinese and non-Chinese citizens are subjected to an annual exchange limit of USD50,000. Exchange will only proceed if the applicant appears in person at the relevant bank, and presents their passport or Chinese ID; these deals are being centrally registered. The maximum dollar withdrawal is USD10,000 per day, and the maximum purchase limit of USD is USD500 per day. This stringent management of the currency inevitably has led to a bottled-up demand for exchange. It is viewed as a major tool to keep the currency peg, but has led to a grey market in USD and an exodus of cash from China, thereby fuelling the boom in Hong Kong property as the Mainland individuals and companies look for a safe repository for their funds.

The country has set its goal to have a fully convertible currency no later than 2028, so I anticipate a continued, straight-line trend of depreciation against the USD over time, albeit with sizeable bumps.

What does this mean for you? Currency fluctuation is a cost of business that you must work around when it comes to producing in China or for the China market, and particularly when negotiating payment terms. From 2014, when the rate was RMB6.2 to USD1, the linear progress to an exchange rate of RMB7.00+ per USD1 seems likely by the end of 2018.

To eliminate the need to hedge against foreign-exchange fluctuations, Chinese vendors are shifting their sights to their domestic market. They no longer need to factor the cost of the USD versus RMB's trading value at some future date. Why wouldn't they prefer doing business at home?

For Westerners, we're competing more and more with the domestic market as the foreign companies we work with look to expand in China to satisfy demand for Western-style goods, albeit made in China, thanks to China's emerging middle class.

Because Chinese exporters negotiate in USD, currency is still a critical part of negotiating. So, it is definitely appropriate to do a deal with a specific margin of exchange rate stipulated, and to allow for recalculation of the dollar-based price if the RMB:USD rate moves 10%+- outside of it. But given the fact that the RMB is not a free-floating currency, and that the Chinese government has shown willingness to "stun" the market and speculators and suddenly change rates, this may help or hinder you. I prefer to stick to my limited area of expertise—sourcing—and leave currency speculation to others who understand it better.

Choosing the Right Structure

There are multiple business structure options to choose from, including equity joint ventures, wholly owned foreign enterprises, representative offices, foreign investment partnerships, and foreign investment entities. My advice is first to choose, by personal recommendation, a good lawyer with offices in both Hong Kong and whichever city in China you are expanding into, who has done this many times before. I have had excellent advice from King and Wood Malleson, but there are others offering a similar service. I have used both wholly owned foreign enterprises and representative offices for running my sourcing and consulting businesses. Each has its pros and cons, but I always ensure they sit under a Hong Kong holding company, which is important to ensure integrity for both legal and accounting matters.

Capital and Dividend Repatriation

Getting profits out of China and understanding the foreign exchange controls is a process that is ever evolving. Beijing is trying to restrict capital leaving China, and as the RMB becomes weaker (an underlying trend), this accelerates as both companies and individuals prefer to own foreign currencies that are not prone to sudden, drastic policy changes. Annual inter-company dividend repayments between affiliates are still a viable structure. But the State Administration of Foreign Exchange now requires approval of transfers over USD5 million, and Chinese firms are encouraged to delay such payments in support of a stronger RMB, so careful planning is essential. Also, note that liquidating an investment in a foreign investment entity takes around 18 months.

Hong Kong versus Shanghai Staff

It's Cheaper in China

Salaries in Hong Kong are more expensive than Shanghai for identical calibre of manager, *but China imposes on the employer a 39% surcharge for "welfare payments",* that the employees believes they will never see, but must be paid, as shown in Table 7.1, hence the similar total cost of employment between the two locations.

PRC Social Insurance Premiums	Employer	Employee
Pension	20%	8.0%
Medical	9.5%	2.0%
Unemployment	0.5%	0.5%
Employment Injury	0.4%	-
Maternity	1.0%	-
Provident Fund	7.0%	7.0%
Total Contribution	38.4%	17.5%

Table 7.1 Social insurance premiums imposed by China
(Source: 55 Consulting 2017)

So, the reason to relocate from Hong Kong to China is more about the *proximity* to production (which has moved dramatically quickly from the south to the north in China) and the *more aggressive attitude* of staff in Shanghai than the cheaper cost. Table 7.2 shows a real-life benchmarking.

Position	Hong Kong			Shanghai, China				HK vs Shanghai Variance (in USD)	HK vs Shanghai Variance (in %)
	Salary/Mth (in USD)	13th Mth Fixed Bonus (in USD)	Total Employment Cost/Annum (in USD)	Salary/Mth (in USD)	13th Mth Fixed Bonus (in USD)	Social Insurance & Provident Fund/Mth (in USD)	Total Employment Cost/Annum (in USD)		
General Manager	11,500	11,500	149,500	8,800	8,800	1,220	129,040	20,460	13%
Senior Manager	7,000	7,000	91,000	5,800	5,800	1,220	90,040	960	1%
Manager	5,100	5,100	66,300	3,200	3,200	1,220	56,240	10,060	15%
Senior Merchandiser	4,100	4,100	53,300	2,600	2,600	1,220	48,440	4,860	9%
Merchandiser	3,200	3,200	41,600	1,850	1,850	800	33,650	7,950	19%
QA Manager	5,600	5,600	72,800	4,800	4,800	1,220	77,040	-4,240	-6%
QC Manager	5,000	5,000	65,000	3,500	3,500	1,220	60,140	4,860	7%
Shipping Manager	4,800	4,800	62,400	3,800	3,800	1,220	64,040	-1,640	-3%

Table 7.2 Salary benchmarking for Hong Kong and Shanghai (Source: 55 Consulting 2017)

Hiring and Firing Flexibility

The two jurisdictions are very different. Hong Kong gives the employer great leeway, and staff can be terminated at short notice with minimal cost, allowing a great deal of flexibility. In contrast, Mainland Chinese staff enjoy much greater government protection, and every termination is a negotiation involving potentially significant payments, or the risk of the member of staff going to the Labour Bureau and starting a long, drawn-out negotiation. The key lesson here is that it is easy to operate in Hong Kong, but it requires experienced human relations management to successfully run an office in China. For my own business, we do not have a human resources manager in Hong Kong, but in Shanghai we have an experienced and competent manager who runs both human resources, and is a certified public accountant, so can oversee the financial aspects of the office. Please factor this in when deciding where to operate.

Fear Factor

After each "crisis" in China, many Western corporations or entrepreneurs relocate production either closer to home or somewhere else. Plain and simple: This isn't a good long-term plan, even though we know how difficult it is to execute a China plan in good times and bad. In good times, there's too much demand and the China side pays less attention to you and has less patience. In bad times, everyone overreacts. Your own team might even dissuade you from including China in your business plan.

You must be a consistent salesperson to convince your team and others around you that China remains a good long-term strategy. It helps to remind yourself of all the China benefits outlined in our earlier Why China? chapter. Remember that the fear factor is worse with people who aren't already working in China because they're only reading headlines that offer a partial reality. Given the unique position of control that the China government has over their country's economy, China gives us the most confidence when it comes to correcting actions and steering their course to sustained success.

As a consultant, I regularly work with CEOs that get very worried about having too much reliance on China. There's stress over social issues or the potential of trade wars. My advice is almost always the same: You must institute a diversification strategy so that you aren't relying on one country, but you can't take China completely out of the equation. It's too large and too good at what it does. Implement a 1+2 strategy to spread your risk, China plus Vietnam and Cambodia, for example. Don't put all your eggs in one basket. But remember that the 1.3 billion population of China can't be swapped with the 90 million in Vietnam or 15 million in Cambodia.

DISRUPTION IS OPPORTUNITY

Consistency breeds complacency. If you are smaller and nimbler than your competition, it is a huge competitive advantage. People will turn to you when change occurs if you become a reliable "go-to" guy for when there's a sudden impact—perhaps a stock market crash, or a currency revaluation, or new legislation, or political upheaval.

Right now, in Hong Kong, large buying agencies are trying to reinvent themselves for the digital age. But as explained elsewhere, there is an increasingly limited niche for a middleman who acts for anyone who will pay for his or her services. Imagine all those customers who are looking for a better, aligned solution to further their margin and secure their supply chains! That is the sweet spot I find so alluring, and it is only available because of change. When things are normal, predictable and "flat", no one has a reason to change. So, learn to adapt your business model, and embrace change.

SUMMARY

- Understand the basis of Chinese law, and how limited it is in support of your commercial rights. In general, the laws are strong but the enforcement sporadic.
- Legal intellectual property protection is theoretically available, but in practice, it is a common-sense approach that relies on relationships with suppliers and staff that provides the most effective protection.
- There is a bewildering range of structures available when you wish to set up a business in Mainland China, and the rules are constantly evolving. *Having a law firm with Hong Kong and China offices that is personally introduced to you with a strong recommendation is a must.*
- Capital and dividend repatriation out of China can be arranged with careful planning and the right structure.

CONCLUSION

> Wisdom is as the moon rises,
> perceptible not in progress but in result.
>
> Chinese proverb

The 6 Secrets are the foundation of everything I have attempted to do and the reason for my success. How you embrace these will define whether your business will succeed in China:

- Generating Trust
- Mastering Negotiation
- Networking with Purpose
- Building your Platform

- Partnering for Profit
- Coping with Challenges

Work your way through all and you will have a wonderful grounding for doing business in China. And please focus on the first one. I believe that it is the Secret of Generating Trust that lies at the heart of your personal brand, and underwrites your performance in negotiating, creating a network, building a platform, and finding partners.

I have been massively fortunate in finding mentors who took me under their wing, and a board of directors who continue to challenge, guide, correct, and provoke me when we meet every quarter. These people have changed my entire approach not just to business, but also to life. This book is my attempt to give back some of what I have been fortunate enough to receive.

Getting on that plane back in 1996 and moving to Hong Kong was the catalyst for me discovering a thoroughly enjoyable business life. I've had lots of failures, made many misjudgements, and taken several wrong turns, but I have no regrets. The rewards have eclipsed the challenges, and that's a fine place to end!

AFTERWORD

> Choose a job you love and
> you'll never have to work a day in your life.
>
> Confucius

My dad was a successful businessman in the north of England. He'd left school at 14, joined the RAF during World War 2, and afterwards put himself through night school to learn design. Starting with nothing, he built up a factory of 700 people making footwear. He raised me to treasure the "northern work ethic"—don't buy what you cannot afford, work hard, save, and invest in property. He believed that education was something that no one could take away from you, so attending the best schools was an investment rather than a cost. But he always regretted not being a CEO of a publicly listed company, and so I inherited his dream and it became my goal from a very early age. I studied economics as early as I could, and always aspired to go into business.

In 2002, when the buying agency I managed successfully floated on the Hong Kong Stock Exchange, my goal was achieved, at the age of 43. Life was filled with annual general meetings, international analysts' meetings, interviews on Bloomberg and CNBC, and profiles in the International Herald Tribune and others. But I felt surprisingly "flat". After working for 23 years I'd achieved my goal; so what was next? I didn't have the same passion to move on to ever bigger companies and balance sheets. What I started to crave was control. I didn't have any problem jumping on a plane at a moment's notice to rescue a deal, or fix a factory output problem for my customers, but I did resent being requested by the board to undertake a variety of fringe projects and political trips. And quarterly reporting was a nightmare for a highly seasonal business such as a buying agency.

I felt like I was a "hired gun" in a town full of entrepreneurs and family business operators. But this relative rarity made me a strong candidate to be recruited into the Young Presidents Organisation, and be fortunate enough to join a forum of like-minded international businessmen who generously shared their experiences. This stimulated me into considering what I really wanted to do with the second half of my business career—and the answer was obvious! Work for myself and be accountable just to myself. Now that I had access to the inner workings of my forum "brothers", I better understood the skillset and risks required. Just as I was hungry for their blend of entrepreneurialism and freedom, they were hungry to learn from my corporate "hired gun" discipline and training. And so, my concept of going out on my own was born. At the same time, I was struggling to set my goals for my new business. How much is enough? In the end, I decided to set myself a challenging goal—

to earn as much a year as I had as a CEO, and to give myself one year to hit this target. (I excluded the value of the many benefits I received as an employee, such as health insurance, stock options, and golf club membership so this wasn't quite the stretch it might appear).

Thanks to my network, and having prepared for over a year before starting, I met my goal immediately. My next year's goal became to have a sufficient pipeline of work to pick and choose what I worked on. In truth, this is still a work in progress, and saying no to potentially arduous clients isn't my strong suit, but I am now in a position to focus more on what I enjoy doing rather than what I feel I must do. Consulting isn't much fun as a short-term gig—all my best decisions have been made when I've had a long-term relationship with a company, whether initially as a consultant who turned into a non-executive director, or a consultant who morphed into the CEO's mentor. Or even as a consultant who transformed into overseeing the Asian sourcing and profitability of my longest running client AquaLeisure, a brand owner and developer of swim and water-related items that dominates their category in a range of US big box retailers.

Running my own business is all about freedom. I work hard but differently, and am always available to my overseas clients. But last night, I attended my daughters' school's phonics workshop to learn how best to support their teachers' methods of practising reading. And in three weeks' time, I can guarantee being at their nativity play (one is playing Mary, the other a sheep!). This was never possible when I was an employee, even when I was the CEO. I never took a vacation that was more than two hours' flight away from Hong Kong in case of emergencies, and was always jumping on planes at no notice. So now, I've traded currencies. Instead of purely focusing on dollars, I've balanced it with a much rarer commodity—time. No one knows how much time he or she has—but you can decide how much money is enough, and how modestly or lavishly you wish to live, and how much you need to set aside for your children's lives after you die. A shroud has no pockets, at least not for physical assets. But the good you can do, and the happy memories you have generated, live on longer.

Don't get me wrong; earning money is a validation of your value and importance. But it's not my only measure of success. You need to control it, rather than have it exert total influence over you.

And that is what I have made in China—a job that is infinitely interesting and stimulating. That I would do even if I wasn't paid, because it is a privilege to be shown inside the workings of my clients' businesses, and be trusted to advise them. My work life has evolved into a series of "case studies", with a reasonable balance that lets me spend more time with my family than I'd ever have thought possible whilst a "hired gun", a chance to resume my passion for painting and teaching my kids art, and an opportunity to write this book and share it with you.

WORKS CITED

INTRODUCTION: WHY CHINA?

1. Eichengreen, Barry and Domenico Lombardi. "RMBI or RMBR? Is the Renminbi Destined to Become a Global or Regional Currency?" *Asian Economic Papers*, MIT Press, vol. 16(1), pages 35-59, Feb. 2017.
2. Goss-Custard, Louise. "The Great APAC Headquartering Debate." *Russell Reynolds Associates*, 2017. www.russellreynolds.com/insights/thought-leadership/the-great-apac-headquartering-debate. Accessed 31 Jan. 2018.
3. Xinhua. "Over 500 Multinationals Set Up Regional Headquarters in Shanghai." *China Daily*, 8 Dec. 2016. europe.chinadaily.com.cn/business/2016-12/08/content_27609354.htm. Accessed 31 Jan. 2018.
4. "Doing Business in China." *King & Wood Mallesons*, 2017. www.kwm.com/en/knowledge/downloads/doing-business-in-china-20170801. Accessed 31 Jan. 2018.

5. "2017 Best Countries to Start a Business." *U.S. News & World Report L.P.*, 2017.
6. Wikipedia contributors. "List of cities in China by population and built-up area." *Wikipedia, The Free Encyclopedia*. Wikipedia, The Free Encyclopedia, 24 Jan. 2018. en.wikipedia.org/wiki/List_of_cities_in_China_by_population_and_built-up_area. Accessed 31 Jan. 2018.
7. Schept, Ken. "BrandZTM Top 30 Chinese Global Brand Builders 2017." *Brandz.com*.
8. Simons, Gary F. and Charles D. Fennig, editors. *Ethnologue: Languages of Asia, Twentieth Edition*. SIL Publications, 2017.
9. Garun, Natt. "Alibaba Singles' Day Sale Amassed $25.3 Billion, Doubling 2016 Black Friday and Cyber Monday Sales Combined." *The Verge*, 11 Nov. 2017. Accessed 31 Jan. 2018.
10. "Doing Business in China." *King & Wood Mallesons*, 2017. www.kwm.com/en/knowledge/downloads/doing-business-in-china-20170801. Accessed 31 Jan. 2018.
11. Lovemoney Staff. "32 Famous Western Brands Bought by the Chinese." *MSN*, 17 Jan. 2017. www.msn.com/en-in/money/photos/32-famous-western-brands-bought-by-the-chinese/ss-AAkGqup?li=AAggbRN. Accessed 31 Jan. 2018.
12. Pooler, Michael. "Robot Army Is Transforming the Global Workplace." *The Financial Times*, 20 Nov. 2017.
13. Weinswig, Deborah. "Alibaba's New Retail Integrates Retail, Store, and Logistics: Is This the Next Gen of Retail?" *Forbes*, 16 Apr. 2017. www.forbes.com/sites/deborahweinswig/2017/04/14/alibabas-new-retail-integrates-e-commerce-stores-logistics-is-this-the-next-gen-of-retail/#52729476767c. Accessed 7 Jan. 2018.
14. *Q4 2017 Retail Sourcing Report*. CBX Software, Nov. 2017.
15. "The Greater Bay Area Initiative." *KPMG and HKGCC*, Sept. 2017.

16. Luo, Wangshu. "More Chinese Students Set to Study Overseas." *The Telegraph*, 21 Mar. 2017. www.telegraph.co.uk/news/world/china-watch/society/more-students-to-study-overseas/. Accessed 31 Jan. 2018.
17. "Innovation Takes Off in China." *Fortune*. Time, 1 Dec. 2017.
18. Wang, Kevin W., et al. "Digital China: Powering the Economy to Global Competitiveness." *McKinsey & Company*, Dec. 2017.
19. "China E-Commerce: The Next Leg of Growth." *Goldman Sachs*, July 2017. www.goldmansachs.com/our-thinking/pages/ronald-keung-china-next-leg-of-growth.html. Accessed 24 Mar. 2018.
20. "China to End One-Child Policy and Allow Two." *BBC*, 29 Oct. 2015. www.bbc.com/news/world-asia-34665539. Accessed 31 Jan. 2018.

SECRET 2: MASTERING NEGOTIATION

1. Fang, Tony. *Chinese Business Negotiating Style*. Sage Publications, 1998.
2. "CNYUSD Spot Exchange Rate." *Bloomberg*. www.bloomberg.com/quote/CNYUSD:CUR. Accessed 31 Jan. 2018.

SECRET 4: BUILDING YOUR PLATFORM

1. Wikipedia contributors. "Websites Blocked in Mainland China." *Wikipedia, The Free Encyclopedia*. Wikipedia, The Free Encyclopedia, 29 Jan. 2018. en.wikipedia.org/wiki/Websites_blocked_in_mainland_China. Accessed 31 Jan. 2018.

SECRET 6: COPING WITH CHALLENGES

1. "2016 Business Climate in China Report." *The American Chamber of Commerce in the People's Republic of China, 2016*. In partnership with Bain & Company.

2. McKern, Bruce and George S. Yip. *China's Next Strategic Advantage: From Imitation to Innovation*. MIT Press, 2016.
3. Wikipedia contributors. "Renminbi." *Wikipedia, The Free Encyclopedia*. Wikipedia, The Free Encyclopedia, 27 Jan. 2018. en.wikipedia.org/wiki/Renminbi. Accessed 31 Jan. 2018.

ABOUT 55 CONSULTING

55 Consulting provides apparel and consumer goods sourcing consultancy to:
- Western retailers, either optimising their existing Asian sourcing offices or setting up their own operations in Asia.
- Private equity firms who want to improve the performance of their investments, specifically if they have a need to improve margins through better sourcing.
- Hong Kong and Chinese factories looking to improve their performance and their understanding of Western customers.

In all cases, benchmarking prices, vendors, and costs allows for the simple assessment of how effective the current operation is and what scope for improvement exists.

After the assessment period is complete, 55 Consulting presents a plan with a timeline for implementation, and typically take responsibility for implementing the plan to the specified benchmarks. This includes:
- Restructuring the organisation chart.
- Hiring the key staff if change is required.
- Training staff.
- Overseeing the new process implementation.

For additional information and client list see www.55brandmgmt.com.

ABOUT THE AUTHOR

Steve Feniger has 30 years' international experience in sourcing, manufacturing, and retailing, the last 20 based in Hong Kong and Shanghai.

He was born and educated in England, graduating from the University of Manchester with an Honours Degree in Management Sciences.

Steve started his career as a management trainee at Marks & Spencer, where he stayed for 18 years as a buying manager in London, Paris, and finally Hong Kong, where he was sent in 1996 to set up direct Asian sourcing.

At the end of three years in Hong Kong, preferring not to move back to London, he resigned to run global sourcing, manufacturing, and retailing for Warnaco Inc. overseeing USD600m annual production of Calvin Klein Jeans, Calvin Klein Underwear, Chaps Ralph Lauren, and Speedo as Senior Vice President.

From 2001 to 2006, Steve was CEO of Linmark Group, then one of the largest buying agencies in Asia, and led a successful IPO on the Main Board of the Hong Kong Stock Exchange in 2002. He managed 1,000 staff across 37 buying offices, spanning 18 different countries across Asia, with hubs in Hong Kong, Bangalore, and Shanghai.

In 2006, Steve left corporate life and established 55 Consulting for retailers to professionalise their approach to Asian sourcing.

Steve has always had a keen interest in supplier social compliance, (balancing the demands of Western retailers with the realities of working in China) and corporate governance. He has lectured on this subject at Beijing University International Law Faculty.

Printed in Great Britain
by Amazon